MW00423585

ADVANCE PRAISE FOR
A Year in the Life of Death

"Shawn Levy has written into the mouth of death with a mission: to reclaim joy, ecstasy, passion, the matter of art. The poems in *A Year in the Life of Death* reanimate those we lost during an unimaginable epoch of loss, and yet, aren't we always living up and through loss? Don't we need to remember how to carry the tune and voice, the art and work, and the bodies of those who are gone? This book is a wailing song, with side eye when and where you need it. These poems are a resuscitation of art and heart."

—**Lidia Yuknavitch**, author of *Verge,*
The Book of Joan, and *The Chronology of Water*

"Shawn Levy's *A Year in the Life of Death* blows past its premise (emanations of one year's *New York Times* obituaries) into a staggering symphony of lives, with parallels to Michael Lesy's *Wisconsin Death Trip* and Jim Carroll's 'People Who Died,' but all the more shocking for having been shared. In the emotional cacophony of the transitional era that seems to have been initiated by 2016, some code seems to be embedded in these losses, and in their reportorial summaries, which only Shawn Levy in his brilliantly angular perspective could have decoded."

—**Ed Skoog**, author of *Run the Red Lights*
and *Travelers Leaving for the City*

"This debut poetry collection seems to me an ode to readership—to the transportive experience made available to a human who picks up a newspaper with an open heart and a broad imagination, ready to treasure the stories of other humans. I'm grateful to Shawn Levy for reminding me what a generous, evocative exchange the newspaper obituary can be."

—**Elena Passarello**, author of
Animals Strike Curious Poses

"Full of feisty and tender elegies, *A Year in the Life of Death* is a sweeping ekphrasis of the American twentieth century. With his gimlet eye and big heart, Levy takes us on a backstage tour of our own popular culture. As much as these poems eulogize and lionize, they also revise and scrutinize, each with a kind of unboxing at the end. The effect is original, and the book exudes that rarest of all qualities in poetry: fun."

—**Dobby Gibson**, author of *Little Glass Planet*

"In this brilliant collection, Levy unfolds portraits within portraits, giving us moving and insightful glimpses of lives embedded in their own cultures and time. His poetry is a striking montage of how we remember, retain, and love through our public mourning."

—**Juan Delgado**, author of *Vital Signs*,
winner of American Book Award

A Year in the Life of Death

A Year in the Life of Death

POEMS INSPIRED by the OBITUARY PAGES
of the *NEW YORK TIMES*

Shawn Levy

UNIVERSITY OF HELL PRESS | PORTLAND, OREGON

HELL PRESS
UNIVERSITY OF HELL PRESS

This book is published by University of Hell Press
www.universityofhellpress.com

© 2021 Shawn Levy

Cover and Interior Design by Gigi Little
gigilittle.com

Published in the United States of America
ISBN 978-1-938753-41-1

*for my teachers and editors, all of 'em,
and in memory of Dominick Vecchiarelli*

TABLE OF CONTENTS

INTRODUCTION

In November 2015, I heard novelist Mo Daviau read a tart and pointed essay inspired by an obituary from *The New York Times* memorializing someone whose treatment at the hands of our larger culture had long vexed her.

I, too, had long thought about this person, and I had clipped that very same obituary and saved it among the myriad similar clippings I'd culled from the *Times* through my 50-ish years of readership. As a sentimentalist and, alas, a ghoul, I've always loved obits, or, as I think of them, brief-lives-of-the-notable-written-on-daily-deadlines. And, as a journalist, I adored writing them—like trailers for biographies. The obits are just about my favorite section of any paper.

As Mo and I chatted, an epiphany: It seemed possible that there might be a prompt for a poem in each day's *Times* obits, and I might try to write such a poem daily for, oh, a year, say the new year that would soon be upon us.

That, of course, was madness. For starters, I don't get the paper every single day: one travels; it snows. And some days the obit pages are simply uninspiring: a Bolivian general, a prize-winning chemist, a Polish ballerina, and not a poem among them.

As it happened, 2016, the year of my project, was the year that *everybody* died: David Bowie, Prince, Merle Haggard, Leonard Cohen, Muhammad Ali, Arnold Palmer, Gordie Howe, Antonin Scalia, Nancy Reagan, Fidel Castro, John Glenn, Janet Reno, Carrie Fisher, Debbie Reynolds, etc. ... a roll call that was also a history of the 20th century.[1] Try writing *that* on deadline.

At the same time, looking at the obits page with a curator's eye, I learned virtually every day of various fascinating lives I'd not known of previously: a woman who starred in a beloved TV commercial; the creators of the Big Mac and General Tso's Chicken; Tupac Shakur's mother; one of the last three Shakers; a rebellious Miss America; the guy who chose the '@' key for email addresses; and so on.

My desire to be authoritative, to write a poem for every truly notable decedent of the year, was overwhelmed by the sheer number of them, as was my wish to pay homage to the amazing little-known lives

---

[1] In January 2017, the *Times* published an article answering the question of whether the previous year was particularly heavy in deaths of notables and concluded, along with editors at the BBC and Legacy.com, that "there was an unusually high proliferation of them in 2016."

my reading had revealed to me. And so, I capped my work load: One hundred poems—a century—would have to do.

Also, to compensate for my weeks of *Times*-lessness, I chose my subjects starting with that first obit—Thanksgiving, more or less, 2015—and running through the end of January, 2017: approximately 365 trips to the end of the driveway for my paper. And, as it happened, the poem-making wouldn't be a daily matter; in fact, it took more than three years to compose and select this group of odes, personal reflections, histories, and jokes. (Yes, jokes: It *is* a book about death, after all.)

A Note on Representation
On March 11, 2018, when I was still composing these poems, *Times* published a remarkable special section entitled "Overlooked: Revisiting 167 years of *New York Times* history to provide obituaries to women who never got them." It acknowledged that the paper's obituary pages had, by a significant preponderance, been dedicated to recording the lives and deeds of Old White Men. As *Times* obituary editor William McDonald noted, acknowledging the gender disparity in its pages, "The … the obituaries desk covers the past, not the present … (Obituaries are) a rear-view mirror, reflecting the world as it was, not as it is, and not as we wish it might have been."

The "Overlooked" section attempted to amend for history—both that of the world and that of the *Times*—by recounting the life stories of exceptional women who had been ignored by the paper at the time of their passing, including, astoundingly, Diane Arbus, Ida B. Wells, Charlotte Brontë, and Sylvia Plath. Less than a year later, the *Times* published a second "Overlooked," focusing on the lives of Black men and women whom it had denied obituaries, including Scott Joplin and Oscar Micheaux. And ever since that first "Overlooked," the *Times'* daily obituary pages have regularly published the life stories of women and people of color whom the paper ignored at the time of their deaths, often decades before their obituaries finally ran.

When I read the *Times'* belated acknowledgements, I recognized that I shared the same cultural biases, and I resolved to correct them. I realized that the 2016 obituary pages were filled with the stories of white men who had, for the most part, made their marks on the world from the 1950s through the 1980s. And I began to look hard at how relatively little a white man had to do to ignite my mind compared to women and people of color. Yes, all the people I would write poems about would have to meet the ineffable criterion of summoning a poem in me. But I could do better. So, I culled and wrote and culled more and wrote more, almost up to the moment of submitting the manuscript for design. In each pass, I made the selection more representative of the *whole* world, and I learned a little more about the lenses of bias to which I had become inured.

I hope that the finished product represents a panoply of life—which isn't to say that it's perfect—

and that it serves as proof of my intention to continue examining the prejudices and assumptions that made such a serious reckoning necessary in the first place. This book is, more than any other I've written, a work of my heart, and as such I hope that it represents the best of me, including my desire to do and see better.

A Note on Format

Each poem ends with the *Times* headline, which includes the deceased's name, age, and noted achievement.[2] In almost all cases, the headline *is* the final line of the poem. I know it's tempting to jump ahead and see whom you're reading about, but try to get there through the flow.

Oh, and this—

SPOILER ALERT

Everybody here dies. Every last one.

2

Headlines appear in these pages exactly as they appeared in the out-of-town edition of the *Times*—the Northwest version, to be precise—and the date cited for each is the date of print publication in that edition. Any inconsistencies in punctuation and format reflect the originals.

Invocation

'Muse' is a shitty job,
Particularly if you're a woman
With a thirst to make art of your own
Whom times and mores insist
Latch on to some man
And fuck him and make him dinner
And drape his arm at functions
And generally vanish, along with your dreams,
Into the cloud
Of his fantasy
Of who you are.

Worse, still, that he was a monster,
Literally stabbed you in the back
After you told him, in front of all New York,
That he was no Dostoyevsky
And had a tiny cock to boot.
"Get away from her," he growled
When they bent to help you
Bleeding on the floor.
"Let the bitch die."

Let. The bitch. Die.

And *his* obit appeared on A-1,
Without naming you for twenty-three paragraphs,
While yours ran on B-11
With him in the headline and the photo.

You made art your whole life,
You made of yourself,

As you dreamed in youth,
A woman "who ate men alive
And spit out the bones,"
And yet you'd always be known,
By name, by repute,
Even at death, as his.

Well, fuck that guy
And his fat books and wee dick and six wives.
Instead, let us sing *you*,
Actor and sculptor and painter,
Who outlived the bastard
And wrote it all down,
The facts of who you were,
In which he was but a chapter,
And raised his two daughters,
Artists the both of them,
Inspired by their mother's example
Independent of their father's fame.

Daughter, mother, lover,
Creator in pith and core,
Not a goddess but a human,
Needing no man for your value,
Inspiring with your resilient
Refusal to be erased,
For which strength and conviction
I call you by the name
You were born with and deserve—
Adele Carolyn Morales—
Because fuck that man

And every man remotely like him,
Spit them out, floss your teeth,
Put on something fabulous,
Grab a brush or pen or hammer,
And fly.

Adele Mailer, 90, Dies; Artist Married Norman Mailer
(November 24, 2015)

I

Page One

He knows where you are
And, more important,
Where you'll be,
And when
He comes, well,
There you go.

You can't avoid him.
Not a dozen
In all the myths of Earth
Have ascended without end,
And they were the likes
Of Hercules, Elijah,
Mary, Simon Magus,
And sundry prophets and swamis.
Not, in short, good odds
For us mortals.

So, you're his, face it.
But only *at* a point
And only *to* a point,
Because, like a sharp,
You can shape the hand he deals you
Into the pieces of a riddle
And turn it back on him.

He'll solve it, know that,
And when he does
He can have you
As you will be had:
Wailing, cowing, ruing, begging, already gone,

Or dancing, laughing,
Dressed like a duke,
With the taste of birthday cake on your lips,
Dropping a big old art bomb
As you slip out from a world
Which will always have you in it
And alive.

*David Bowie, Star Whose Fame Transcended Music, Dies
at 69* (January 12, 2016)

As if I could capture you on paper
When men dead-set and strong and fleet
Couldn't in the flesh,
When the federal government
Couldn't, its might amassed,
When *you yourself* couldn't
When playing *you yourself* on film.
You were, just as you said,
Too speedy, too pretty, too great:
A lightning rod, an emblem,
A talking point, a star
Shining well beyond the couple
Hundred square feet
From within which
You vanquished the world.
The gifts you were accorded;
The work to husband them;
The obstacles thrown at you;
How you danced through them all;
The heights you mounted;
The punishments you stood;
The diversion you offered;
The lessons you taught;
Medals; belts; money;
Showmanship; the life itself:
Could it all have happened
To make us watch the finale,
To see you—tall, fit, handsome, strong—a torch
In your hand, not to burn
Things down but to light
A flame above the games

At which you once became,
And not for the last time, supreme?
You shook then with disease,
From which, as with foes in the ring,
As with the army and FBI,
As with critics of your words and creed
And sporting mien and very skin,
You simply would not back away,
And showed us what it was to be
A man, indeed, a champion:
The greatest, yes, but also the most
Humble, the most human, the most real.

Muhammad Ali, 1942-2016, The Champ Who Transcended Boxing (June 5, 2016)

I see you on your knees before
A teacher, lover, tape recorder, desk,
An emblem of serene humility
(A thought you'd no doubt deem a vanity).

I saw you once for real, in my home town,
In twain, in fact—not only in the flesh
But on a giant screen. Indeed: in threes:
Your shadow huge on cobalt scrims behind you.

And I've spied you in places you never were:
The temples of Black Rock City;
The light on waterfalls and mists;
The eyes of a certain woman;
Some words drilled into my arm in ink.

It's a measure of your weight for me
That the more I think about you,
The more I think about you,
And I esteem you as a holy man
As often as a poet, imp, roué,
Sensei, comedian, wandering Jew,

All of which you were, and which names
You'd no doubt lay claim to sooner
Than you would the hero's crown
I hold above your head—
Which makes me love you all the more.

Leonard Cohen, Poet and Songwriter of 'Hallelujah,' Dies at 82 (November 12, 2016)

You topped your profession for years—
Sixty times in total,
Seven on the biggest stages of all—
Earning thirty million dollars
And the love of the world,
With a grin and a swagger
And one of those names
Simply coined to be famous,
And still, you'll likely best
Be remembered for a moment
When, frozen with indecision
That never seemed to strike you
When it counted, you couldn't
Choose between the simplest things.

All those hours of practice,
All that competition, all that talent,
World fame, universal respect, a whole life,
And a guy winds up immortal
For mixing lemonade
And iced tea in a glass.

Arnold Palmer, 87, Face of Golf, Dies
(September 27, 2016)

It happens every day, realtalk:
People die from broken hearts.
Spouses; after fifty, sixty years:
One goes, and the other,
Befuddled,
Cut in half,
A bit later:
Life and love
Rounded off
In weeks, months.

But why make
A miniseries
Of a two-act play?
Why not cap off
A grim year's
Butcher's bill
With a bang?

And so:
A daughter takes ill,
Lingers four days,
Then succumbs,
And her mother,
Mere hours later—
And just as out of
Nowhere—as well:
Curtain.

They had their differences
But couldn't,

In the end,
Be apart,
And, divas in their bones,
They pulled off
A boffo ending
No screenwriter
Would ever dream of pitching,
Not even stewed to the gills.

Carrie Fisher, 1956-2016: In a Film Princess, Fame's Light and Dark Sides (December 28, 2016)

Debbie Reynolds Dies at 84; Won Hearts of Generations (December 30, 2016)

All deaths
In a sense
Are one.
But in the news game
One death
Sometimes
Eclipses all.

You may be
Many things
In life:
Football star,
Federal DA,
Orchestra conductor,
Baseball historian.

But die on the same day
As a former First Lady
And what you are
In the end
Is filler.

Al Wisbert, a Tenacious All-Pro Tackle for Championship Eagles Teams, Dies at 95; Robert Del Tufo, 82, Ex-Federal Prosecutor; Nikolaus Harnancourt, Conductor and Early Music Specialist, Dies at 86; Tom Knight, 89, Knew It All About Brooklyn Baseball

Nancy Reagan, 1921-2016, Fierce Protector and Influential Force as First Lady

(March 7, 2016)

"Of the dead
Nothing but good
Is to be said."
—Chilon of Sparta,
Philosopher,
600 B.C.

"I'll be glad
When you're dead,
You rascal you."
—Sam Theard,
Songwriter,
1929

"I have never
Killed anyone,
But I have read
Some obituary notices
With great satisfaction."
—Clarence Darrow,
Lawyer,
1932

"His own
Worst enemy?
Not while
I'm alive
He's not."
—Walter George,
Congressman,
1938

"If you can't say
Something nice
About someone,
Then don't say
Anything
At all."
—Everyone's mom,
Ever

Justice Antonin Scalia Is Dead at 79
(February 14, 2016)

When my dad went,
I was three thousand miles away,
Watching a movie
About a sailboat race
With my sons in my lap;
I stood up to answer
A call from my sister,
And she told me,
And I fell to the floor.

For my mom, I kept vigil
In the hospice ward
Of Maimonides,
Hours on hours awake
With coffee, stairway sprints,
Angry Birds. I dozed
Maybe three minutes,
No more,
Roused, and went
To splash cold water
On my face,
And when
I returned,
She was gone.

Those moments
Sparked no bulletins,
Stopped no presses,
Interrupted no programming,
But they're chiseled
In my brain

And I relive them,
Without warning,
Day or night,
My heart
Sinking and racing
At once, a hole
Rent in my life—
Balance lost,
The world
Lopsided,
An amputee,
Unlimbed.

The passing of heroes
Imprints the same way.
The flow of life
Stops; bereft, we gasp,
Crumble, recollect
The stalwart
Who shone above,
Beyond us,
And has,
In a heartbeat,
Vanished.

We forever recall
The moment—
"Where were you when ...?"—
And how it was
We learned.
And the sharing

Of the news
Becomes
A kind of currency:
A way to knit
One to another
Through the agency
Of telling, even
When the message
Is a blow: a kind
Of drama- or
Sensation-porn
For which I confess
A particular
Predilection.

And so, when the
Unthinkable word
Came from Minnesota,
And I called my love—
At her workplace,
No less—to announce
That her favorite artist
Had succumbed,
My call itself was such
A shock that rather
Than feel her natural grief,
She was vexed,
And rightly so,
At my blindness
To her sorrow.

I wish I'd kept my peace.
I wish I'd let a thing
That was bound to hurt
Take her as
And where it might,
And though I know
Now better,
And have done better since,
That misstep
Twined itself in her loss,
A trespass I can't revoke,
An added pain
I can never soothe,
As I well know,

Having never watched
That sailing film again
And determined never
Once more to set foot
In that damn hospital.

Prince, 1958-2016: A Singular, Meticulous Master of Pop
(April 22, 2016)

II

Below the Fold

Afterward, when they'd moved on,
And we could hear their voices,
Independent, one by one,
The gist of each was clear,
But something, too, was missing,
And is it too much to wonder
If what that was was … *you*?
Van Gogh had no collaborators,
Joyce wrote in bed alone,
But popular music is made, if not
By committee, communally,
And that community can stretch beyond
The faces on a stage or album sleeve.
That alchemy, that quintessence,
Required, in this case, a literal fifth,
Which would be you, the grown-up in the room,
The one whose sounds they'd grown up on,
Who helped them shape the unimagined
And gave their fantasies analog form,
And who would, in ways, remain
More devoted to what they'd done than any of them.
You were beside them from the first
Almost to the very last, and the things you did
Together—all of you—were impossible
Until you did them, with pieces of each
And the chemistry of all.
The fifth of four you may have been,
But also, in more than a manner
Of speech, the first and last.

George Martin, Producer Who Guided the Beatles, Dies at 90 (March 10, 2016)

That it's all make-believe
Makes it no less unfair
To be deprived the spotlight
One creates with one's voice.

Anna swooning with her king,
Maria primping for Tony,
Eliza bending vowels for her love—
You brought life to their songs

Even as the women with their faces
Won the prizes and the glory,
Becoming iconic, in part,
Thanks to the sound you made in the shadows.

You were, for want of a term of art,
A ghost singer, treated gratefully, one hopes,
By Misses Kerr and Wood and Hepburn,
But uncredited, by contract and by threat.

And when time came to set
The story down, on paper, to tell all,
You did the decent thing, the thing
That had been denied you all along,

And gave the fellow
Who helped write your memoir
Equal billing
On the title page.

Marni Nixon, the Singing Voice Behind the Screen, Dies at 86 (July 26, 2016)

It is no easy thing to be a son,
Much less a namesake,
Much less to a king,
Much less in his wake.

If he'd been looking out for you,
The old man would've sent you off to school,
Insisted you master your own field,
Only allowed you near the business
On the backstage side.

But that wasn't how it went.

You sang his songs,
You grew into his face,
You conducted his band,
You bore his name.
Eighteen years you outlived him
But he was there every minute,
Senior to your junior,
Ideal to your aspirant,
Father to your gifts and agonies—
The acme of your affect,
Only getting further from you
The nearer you approached him.

Frank Sinatra Jr., 72, Dies; Followed Father's Footsteps
(March 18, 2016)

In the dining hall of a seniors' home
In May 2016,
Patty Ris, age eighty-seven,
Choked on a bite of lunch.
She was saved by the intervention
Of a ninety-six-year-old fellow resident,
Who wrapped his arms
Around her from behind,
Made a fist above her navel,
And thrust up sharply, dislodging
A piece of meat and clearing her throat.
That particular form of rescue
Had prevented, by some estimates,
One hundred thousand deaths,
But that was the first and only time
It had been executed in practice
By the man who dreamed it
Up and gave it its name.
Seven months later he passed,
An inveterate tinkerer satisfied
That the most famous inspiration of his brain
Worked just as he conceived it would in life.

Henry J. Heimlich, of Famed Maneuver, Dies at 96
(December 18, 2016)

He grabbed you and he kissed you, just like that.
He didn't ask permission or your name,
And it was broad daylight, and there were witnesses,
And one had a camera and caught the whole thing,
And the evidence went around the world.

But evidence of what?
He grabbed you and he kissed you, *maybe*.
Because, first of all: *Was it you*?
At least two others said it was *them*,
And, for that, at least eleven claimed to be *him*.

And what happened, really? The two of you
(If it *was* you) in uniform,
A bubble of euphoria,
The crossroads of the world,
He grabbed you and he bent you back and kissed you,
And in the moment it passed for glee
But decades on it looks like an attack:
A man—in military garb, no less—
Grappling a woman whose eyes are closed,
One hand spread on her left hip,
The other balled up near her head,
Her arms and body limp—
A blend of violence and passivity,
The very picture of sexual assault.

This much is clear: A sailor grabbed a nurse
On V-J Day in Times Square
And leaned her back and kissed her,
And Alfred Eisenstaedt of *Life*,
A Jew from Germany,
Snapped a shot but failed to catch their names,
And though the photo won great fame
You didn't see it for twenty years,
After which you stood and said
You were the girl—

A Jew from Austria, your parents dead
At Hitler's hands, your siblings fled
To Palestine, alone in America
Six years by then, at work
In a dentist's office, wandering
The crowd that day, twenty-one,
Relieved the worst was past.

He grabbed you and he kissed you,
And maybe it was you, and maybe not,
And who knows who he was,
And though you saw there could be some
Affront in what he'd done,
You claimed none: "It was just
Someone celebrating," you said, and,
"It wasn't a romantic event," you said, and,
"I wasn't kissing him, he was kissing me."

And so: Some guy grabbed a girl and kissed her,
And maybe it was okay
With her, and maybe it wasn't,
And one conflict came to an end,
And another, in which that photo looks
Less like a moment of armistice
Than an act of war, still wages.

Greta Friedman, 92, Said to Be Nurse in Iconic Kiss, Dies
(September 11, 2016)

Why should we doubt
The most basic cliché
When we know
Such things rise
From the truth?

No pain compares
To the loss of a child,
Even when
The parent
Is pretend.

Patty Duke, Oscar and Emmy Winner Who Began as a Child Star, Dies at 69 (March 30, 2016)

William Schallert, 93, Dies; Played 'Patty Duke' Father (May 10, 2016)

Prolificacy or perfection: two
Faces of one coin or opposing ideals?

Picture a set of scales with, on one side,
A single volume, slender, resonant, and true,

And, on the other, a towering pile of texts
Produced by a single fecund wizard.

You might expect that gravity or sheer
Brute weight would tip things toward the larger mass.

But it's a mystery of art and life
That they can hover equally and still.

Nelle Harper Lee, 1926 – 2016; 'Mockingbird' Author, Elusive Voice of the Small-Town South

Umberto Eco, Semiotics Scholar Who Became a Best-Selling Novelist, Dies at 84

(February 20, 2016)

Inside every diva:
A debutante
Facing a phalanx
Of impresarios,
Buffs, and critics
Who'd just as soon
Eat her alive
As make her a star.

At eighteen, blind with confidence
That coaxed her family to move
From Spokane to Manhattan,
One such mounted the Met stage
Wearing a lucky ring and crown
And sang a tough role well enough
That the ticket-buyers cheered,
Even as some purists sniffed.

Seven years later, a second soprano,
Only twenty, was phoned at three
And told that at seven she'd perform
A part she'd never sung, the first
Of five hundred plus times her five-two frame
Would command the whole of the Met.

Decades of singing—
Operas, of course,
TV shows, commercials,
Musical theater, films,
A Vegas nightclub gig or two,
A visit with Big Bird—

And all of it rooted
In two moments a few years apart
But near-duplicate in kind:

A girl behind a curtain;
An orchestra clearing its throat;
The press honing their instruments;
The boxes filling with cognoscenti;
A future on the lip of being born.

Patrice Munsel, a Soprano Who Made Her Met Debut As a Teenager, Dies at 91 (August 11, 2016)

Roberta Peters, Who Entered Opera Dramatically, Dies at 86 (January 20, 2017)

A kid exploring galaxies
Of music, I scorned
Anything 'country,'
'Western,' 'honky-tonk,'
And "Okie from Muskogee,"
So hateful of cultures
I subscribed to,
Was all I thought
I needed know of you.

But heroes of mine—
Jerry Garcia, John Doe—
Found treasure in your work,
And, in time, the point
Of Hank Williams, George Jones,
Willie Nelson, Buck Owens, and, yes, you
Revealed itself to me:
The plangent melodies,
The fealty to roots, the voices
Of the voiceless, a sound
Peculiar to this land:
Heroic tenor, raw guitar,
Homey lyrics. I even went so far
As take my sons to see you.
Your music hadn't changed
One drop; I had.

And then, a few years on,
With so many of your songs
In me, I heard you tell
A radio man about "Okie"

And its cry against,
Of all things, marijuana:
"I was dumb as a rock
When I wrote that song,"
You said. "I can't see the word
'Prohibition' and the word
'Freedom' in the same sentence,"
Much as I can't imagine
So much music that I love
Or even the country that so
Awes and vexes me
Without you straddling both,
A colossus with the plainest of ways and miens.

Merle Haggard, 1937-2016, Country Music Outlaw and
Poet of the Common Man (April 7, 2016)

The first thing that needs saying
Is: You both could ball.
Even if the games you played
Were unalike, if your roles,
Your uniforms, your arenas,
Could never be confused,
Each of you was dead serious
About your sport, no matter
The face you showed the crowd.

But you each, too, knew your role:
Star or backup, center stage
Or risers in the rear,
Spinning, standing still,
In the spot, or to the side,
Globetrotter or Pip,
"Sweet Georgia Brown" or
"Midnight Train to Georgia" —

You do the work, hit the notes,
Give the people what they paid for,
And when your team wins, you win,
Even when the game is rigged
Whether for you or against you,
Even if they all know your name best,
Or they don't know your name at all.

Meadowlark Lemon, 1932-2015; Master of Hook Shots and Comedy

William Guest, 74, Longtime Voice with Gladys Knight and the Pips

(December 29, 2015)

Yeah, yeah, we know:
You saw it coming.
Happy?

Youree Dell Harris, 53, TV's Psychic Miss Cleo
(July 27, 2016)

It's hardly the most woke of names.
'Troubled' or 'challenged' or 'differently-abled'
Would all be preferred nomenclature.
Besides which, after what you did—
Embezzlement, skimming, smuggling,
Racketeering, perjury, fraud—
The only "crazy" you could claim to be
Was the kind like a fox
Caught in a henhouse
With its mouth full of feathers.

Eddie Antar, Retailer and Felon Who Created Crazy Eddie, Dies at 68 (September 12, 2016)

Coincidence may be
The definition of life,
And accident, perhaps,
The essence of the news,
But you needn't be
Sherlock Holmes to suspect
That two deaths in one squad room
In such short succession
Is a case worth summoning
Lieutenant Columbo to probe
Or, at the very least, OSHA.

Abe Vigoda, Actor Who Hit His Stride as Mobster in 'The Godfather,' Dies at 94 (January 26, 2016)

Ron Glass, 71, Dapper Detective on 'Barney Miller' (November 27, 2016)

You knew what you were doing,
That much is clear.
From the outside, it could look
Like comedy, chaos even:
A diplomat, a hotelier,
An actor, a banker, an oilman,
A lawyer, a toy maker (toy maker!),
Another actor (one day only,
And at sea!), and, for longer
Than the others all combined,
A self-dubbed prince with a paid-for title.
Madness, on the face of things;
Profound impatience, at the very least.
But each was a step in a progress
For which you even left a map:
Not one, not two, not three,
But *four* books to explain
Where you were coming from
And what you did
To get to where you went.
Hidden out in the open,
Right there on the page:
Your secrets, guileless, free.
You gave yourself away
With such prodigality
To husbands, it was no stretch,
I guess, to do the same for readers.
And as one who read all four—
For research, I swear!—
I confess to being more
Than just a little charmed

By the whole project,
If not a hundred percent convinced
That we needed know so much about it.

Zsa Zsa Gabor, Oft-Married Actress and Film Femme Fatale, Dies at 99 (December 19, 2016)

After three full days
Tromping wastelands,
Banging around
In an ATV,
Digging up rocks and dirt,
Climbing peaks,
Staring into craters,
And tracing
Your daughter's name
Into the dust,
You'd had it.

Strapped in a capsule,
You flipped switches,
Pushed buttons,
Braced for the thrust
And uttered
The last words yet heard on the moon,
Not as famous as the first
But equally poetic
In their way
And no doubt more heartfelt:
"Let's," you said,
"Get this mother out of here."

Eugene A. Cernan, Who Took Humanity's Last Steps on the Moon, Dies at 82 (January 17, 2017)

III

The Arts

"Tragedy is when
I stub my toe,"
Mel Brooks once said.
"Comedy is when
You fall into
An open manhole
And die."

You knew that better than most,
Making satires
On the watches
Of Stalin and Khrushchev,
Tiptoeing a line between
Laughs and tears,
Where one misstep
Could bring an avalanche
Down on your head.
"Sad comedies," you called them.

Today, as I bent
To pick up the paper
That brought word of your death,
My back went out.

I'm guessing you
Would have loved that.

*Eldar Ryazanov, 88; Famed Russian Director Was a
Master of Satire* (December 1, 2015)

I can't say how many times I've seen you—
Twenty, easy, maybe thirty—
And each time it's like the first.

Rebuffed by a man,
Too deep in your cups to be alone,
You're sent home under guard
Only to return the following night
On the arm of a villain.
And then the music starts
In that most musical of non-musicals
And despite your new companions
You reveal your deepest self,
A tear descending a cheek,
Your true native melody
Breaking your heart as you sing it:
La Marseillaise.

You were only nineteen then,
Soon to be divorced
And done with the business of pretend,
But we'll always have
Those indelible minutes
In a barroom in Morocco,
Which was really Burbank,
Or, more precisely, everywhere on Earth.

Madeline Lebeau, 92, 'Casablanca' Actress
(May 17, 2016)

If you're gonna do a thing just once,
Do it so it lasts.

Two lines, throwaways, in a kid director's debut—
The whole of your film career—

And you didn't even get a credit for it.
But the movie endured and likely will

Even longer than you, which, as you
Passed just shy of a hundred and one, is saying plenty.

Kathryn Popper, 100, Dies; Appeared in 'Citizen Kane'
(March 9, 2016)

There is the kind who has one kind to play.
There is the kind who plays all kinds.
And there is the kind who *is* or *has* it:
Character, that is: Character actor.

A side, a garnish, an amuse-bouche,
Adding texture, flavor, spice,
But in smaller, finer doses
Than the names at the head of the dish,

One of those faces you can
Almost place but often mistake,
Seen a hundred times
Yet not attached to any concrete memory,

Not a warranty of quality, not a draw,
But, in regularly mounting appearances,
A rock, a reliable touchstone,
A welcome sight—even,

You might say, a friend.

Robert Loggia, 85, Rugged but Versatile Character Actor
(December 5, 2015)

*Fritz Weaver, 90, Character Actor Who Won a Tony Award
in 1970* (November 28, 2016)

Capone and Gotti and Vinny the Chin
All knew it, and some politicians, too:
You have to dress the part,
You have to walk the walk,
You have to own it, sell it, be it.
So, why not, when the avenues
You've made your living on are closed to you,
Take a crooked path the world deems straight?
Actor, gangster, showman, thug:
What matter if the razor at your throat is just a prop?

Noburo Ando, 89, Mobster and Film Star in Japan Dies
(December 27, 2015)

'Schlockmeister' they called you,
But 'meister' all the same,
And you no doubt
Reveled in the term,
Keen as you were
On the distinguishing note,
To wit that 'Gordon,'
Utterly superfluous
In a town and a business
In which no one else would dare
Own up to being a 'Herschell.'

Herschell Gordon Lewis, 90, Pioneer of Gore Cinema
(September 28, 2016)

If that really was your job description, well,
Whatever they were paying you
It wasn't enough.

Dude: You fucking *killed* it.

Tony Barrow, Beatles' First Publicist, Dies at 80
(May 17, 2016)

To heft a legacy through time—
Anyone's—was never on your list.
You were born to set fire to things,
To break them, make them change.

Yet the child you birthed and nurtured
Commanded the world and still does
Twenty years after he was gunned down
And left you, with your own demons
To fight off and your own dreams
Unfulfilled, to be a mother once again,
This time to a message, not a man,
And carry forward what was left behind.

The genius that you bore to life became
Your own most revolutionary cause.

Afeni Shakur, 69, Guidepost for Rapper Son
(May 4, 2016)

"Too short, too fat,
Too Black, too old"—
That's what they said
When they turned you away
From the stages
And record labels
Where you tried—
No, *demanded*—
To have your voice heard.

But even though their ears
Should forever be suspect
(Or should suspect their brains
For ignoring what they witnessed),
Their greater failing was in their eyes:
They couldn't see inside you,
Where, despite your mammoth voice
And fireball dance steps,
Your greatest gifts—
Resilience, determination,
Patience, hunger, guts—
Lay in such ample supply
That when, in your forties,
You were finally granted
The mic, the spotlight,
You gripped them hard enough
To wring out every drop of life
And put a sound into the world
That no one could ignore.

They should have known, those fools,
When you showed up to cut records
In your prison guard uniform,
When you left your hotels before dawn
On show days to go fishing,
When you played concerts bald
After chemotherapy,
That you were tough enough
And cool enough and strong enough
And damned sure ready enough
To, when you finally got your turn,
Do what it was you always did,
Miss Sharon Jones: You made it yours.

Sharon Jones, Soul Singer With Dap-Kings, Dies at 60
(November 20, 2016)

Even now, learning your age
And the whole arc of your career,
On listening yet again to my two
Favorites of the albums you made,
(One nearly forty years old,
And how does *that* happen?),
On considering a life I knew
Only through snapshots of fandom,
I still imagine you most vividly,
The way I've always seen you:
As the eldest of a trio,
In a basement in New Jersey,
Singing, laughing, teasing,
Having a blast with your sisters,
Weaving your voices (and here
I must confess I never knew
Which was yours and which
Terre's or Suzzy's, though you,
I'm told, were bottommost)
With brio, pathos, savoir faire,
Caroling, mocking, riding waves,
Creating braids the muses
Would set aside their knitting to enjoy,
A sound that carried you all
Into the world, and which I've carried
All these years and passed along
To anyone I've ever loved or wished
To grant a shiver of delight.

Maggie Roche, Who Harmonized With Her Two Sisters,
Dies at 65 (January 23, 2017)

A coin toss: heads or tails.
You're twenty-seven years old — *that number!* —
And there's one seat on the plane.
You win, you fly; you lose, you take the bus.
It comes up tails (or was it heads?)
And the Mexican kid from LA gets your spot.

For fifty-eight years you would wonder
What force made that coin land as it did.
You and Waylon Jennings, riding through the night,
On a cold, dark bus, watching the storm,
Both in Buddy Holly's band, both left behind
When the pilot took a hard turn to oblivion.

Buddy, the Big Bopper, and Ritchie Valens —
Who won that coin toss — gone,
And you left to marry, raise your kids,
Build a career, even get inducted
Into Oklahoma's Music Hall of Fame,
All on the back of a fifty-fifty shot.

Call it fortune, call it fate, call it a blessing,
Or, like you did that night in Iowa,
Call it in the air, and live with your choice.

Tommy Allsup, 85, Guitarist with Luck
(January 16, 2017)

In a barbershop in Jersey City
Your dad, cutting hair,
Suggested you take up the banjo,
And, one way or another,
You wound up on guitar,
Providing the soundtrack
To a million little boys'
Cowpoke dreams:
The themes of both
Bonanza and
The Magnificent Seven.

Is it too much to wonder
If that barbershop was maybe
In *West* Jersey City?

Al Caiola, 96, Guitarist with Range
(November 25, 2016)

It's a pretty good guess
But a guess nonetheless:

No one saw the Big Bang
And lived to tell the tale.

But you accompanied a king
When he wasn't yet a prince

And made a sound so huge
It broke apart a world.

Scotty Moore, 84, Guitarist Who Backed Elvis Presley
(June 30, 2016)

Take all the fucks
Dean Martin could muster
In eighty-eight years
And maybe—*maybe*—
You could fill a rocks glass.
And you? I'm thinking
Demitasse spoon, tops.
You made slick and smug a craft—
In your obit they actually
Called you "annoying"—
But you looked and sounded
Pretty great doing it
(Or not, as the case may be)
And left the stage
Just as you took it:
On your terms,
In your time,
So what can I say but
"Good for you, pallie,
Good for you."

Buddy Greco, Singer Who Had That Swing, Dies at 90
(January 13, 2017)

In the Donbass War of 2014,
A machine-gunner in the trenches,
Who wore his hair in a mohawk
And called himself Meph,
A guy who could sing arias
Or load a gun in time to a folk tune,
Was killed by sniper fire at dawn
Near the town of Debaltseve.
He was forty-one.

The singing was special. Meph was short
For Mephistopheles, from Gounod's *Faust*,
Which role he had sung with honor
At the Paris Opera, where he was a baritone.
He was Ukrainian, born in Lviv,
A prodigy who moved to the West as a teen
And won prizes for his "Toreador Song."
When his people rose against the Russians,
He left the heights he'd sung himself to
For the minefields and barbed wire,
Where he enthralled comrades with
Renditions of "Moon in the Sky,"
Which they'd all been raised to sing.

Is there any part of this that couldn't
Have happened two hundred years ago?
That doesn't sound like an Oscar-season release?
That wouldn't spark the imagination of Stendhal?
But every bit of it was just like that: all true.
A boy with gifts; a man out of time; an artist; a war;
A tribal impulse; a legend in fatigues; a sneak attack;

A fatal reckoning at break of day:
File it under the category
'Crazy Shit That Actually Happened.'

Wassyl Slipak, 41, Paris Opera Baritone
(July 1, 2016)

I never read a line you wrote
Save one, which I love,
And not only was it never published
But it got you fired from writing copy
For the Jolly Green Giant
Who couldn't see the genius
Of the straight and true avowal
In the ad you'd dummied up:
"These are the best
Fucking peas I ever ate."

Thom Jones, Janitor Turned Eminent Author, Dies at 71
(October 19, 2016)

Aging musicians play greatest hits forever.
Athletes getting on in years can coach.
And for actors there's always Miss Havisham or Lear.

But what of the surgeon
Whose hand starts to quiver,
Whose eyesight grows fuzzy,
Who feels the waning of his
Sharpness, dexterity, nerve?

There's only one cure for such a case:
Start to write, as you did at fifty-eight,
Stating plainly, "I didn't want
To hurt anybody."

Even near death, a famed author
Of thirty years tenure,
You chose the gentle path:
"I just want to be cremated
And blow in the wind,"
You told a journalist.

"Too late!" your missus said,
And she was right:
You'd promised your body to science.
A man of medicine, in your bones, to the end.

Richard Selzer, 87, Spun Tales from Surgery
(June 6, 2016)

Remember the great Keats Bio War of '64,
When poets, scholars, critics, juries
Lined up and took sides,
Some with the mighty Bate
And his minute-by-minute tome,
Others with the upstart Ward
And her plumbing of the psyche writ in water?

Such heady times! A Pulitzer to the old pro,
The National Book Award to the kid.
Come to think, it's no surprise
That only three years later they invented
The Super Bowl, clearly inspired
By the fury of this tilt.

Poets, after all, may be
The antennae of the race,
But those who write their lives
Are the radio operators
Who make the invisible intelligible
For the rest of us.

Aileen Ward Dies at 97; Biographer of John Keats
(June 9, 2016)

*"I like plots and stories and well-made plays," Mr.
Dickinson told The Guardian in 1971. "I dream in
plots, and have been known to wake up shouting,
'I simply will not dream these dreadful cliches.'"*

'I simply will not dream these dreadful cliches.'
And no one could blame a plot-maker so screaming.

A dream is a portal to whole worlds unfathomed
And not to a hallway that leads to one door.

We sleep not to know but to feed on not knowing,
To reckon with mysteries sunk in our heads.

The point's not to build to mathematical rigor
But rather to rouse some rough beast we can't tame.

So, bless you for shouting your need to dream wildly,
For having no truck with the dull and the plain.

Awake, we've got all the routine we can stomach.
Our dreams ought to feed us a banquet arcane.

*Peter Dickinson, Author, Dies at 88; Master Plotter
Relished a Good Puzzle* (December 18, 2015)

in the
silence of
monastic
life,
a voice
can find
its way
into
the world
through
hand,
pen,
slice
of paper,
alphabet,
devotion
to form,
precision
of motion,
lines
laid
down
without
regard
to self,

the soul
expressed
in act,
not result,
mastery
as absence,
humility,
service,
beauty,
the word
made word,
its form
its own
end.

Robert Palladino, a Master Calligrapher, Is Dead at 83
(March 6, 2016)

Thin lines,

        Crosshatches,

                Shades, shadows,

        Even blobs

Of watercolor,

          And, of course,

                The words:

        Quips, puns,

Allusions,

          Nods, winks

                      That even a kid

                  On whom

Updike, McPhee, and Kael were wasted

                Could get.

                    The old joke goes,

        'I only look at *Playboy*

For the articles,'

        But the no-lie reason

                  To let all those *New Yorkers*

        Pile up in the corner

Is so very often your cartoons,

                For which relief much thanks.

William Hamilton, Longtime Cartoonist at the New Yorker Who Poked at the Rich, 76 (April 11, 2016)

Frank Modell, 98, Longtime New Yorker Cartoonist, Dies (May 30, 2016)

Anatol Koransky, 97, New Yorker Cartoonist (June 14, 2016)

Michael Crawford, 70; Wielded a Wiseacre Pen (July 15, 2016)

Robert Weber, New Yorker Cartoonist, Is Dead at 92 (November 3, 2016)

'Mind your teachers,'
We tell our kids,
And it's good advice,

And then some clod
In front of a classroom,
Blind to what's before him,

Tells *you*, of all pupils,
"Don't illustrate talking
Animals wearing clothes,"

And you wonder
Why we bother
With school at all.

Peggy Fortnum, 96, British Illustrator of Paddington
(April 10, 2016)

John Adams gasped
"Thomas Jefferson survives"
And died, unaware
That his frenemy
Had, too, expired
Some five hours prior.

Almost two hundred years later,
A woman who sang folk and rock
Passed the same day as the fellow
Who, in their youth, had bid her
Join a revolutionary band known,
For opaque reasons, as Jefferson Airplane.

No record was shared of her final words,
But the ones she said on stage
In her last gig with the group,
Which she left to have a baby,
Would have done nicely once again
If she'd thought of them:

"I want you all to wear smiles
And daisies and box balloons.
I love you all. Thank you,
And goodbye."

Signe Anderson, 74, Jefferson Airplane Singer

Paul Kantner, a Founder of Jefferson Airplane, Dies at 74

(January 29, 2016)

Three songs in,
The band full boil,
Five dancers working it,
The crowd on fire,
On live TV,
In your red bucket hat
And a white shirt
Twined with black snakes,
You slumped,
Your heart
Gone out:
A final beat
No one heard
Amid
The joyous noise.

Papa Wemba, Magnetic Congalese Tenor and 'King of Rumba Rock,' Is Dead at 66 (April 26, 2016)

How much truth do we want?
How many illusions can we bury?
When are frank and honest too damn much?

Sometimes we want the magic, the lie.
Sometimes we want to stay ignorant.
Sometimes we just don't want to know.

"Frosted Lucky Charms,
They're magically delicious!"

I didn't believe that as a kid,
Much less today.
But to learn you weren't Irish,
That you were Dutch-English,
From *Staten Island*:
Well, that's a bowl of truth
I didn't need to eat.

Arthur Anderson, 93, Voice of Leprechaun
(April 14, 2016)

A final moment
On a hazy beach:
Hunched
In the sand,
Knees up,
Covered
By an
Orange
Blanket,
Cocooned
In an
Oatmeal
Sweater,
Arms
Akimbo,
Hands
Clasped,
Hair
Wind-tossed,
Lips
Pursed,
Eyes
On you,
A pro
To the last.

"This one's
For you,
George,"
She said,
In that voice
That staggered
Hearts and loins,
And still does half
A century
After you
Snapped her
Valediction.

George Barris, 94, Dies; Took Last Marilyn Monroe Shot
(October 5, 2016)

Fifty-five times they knocked you out;
Seventeen times they shot you.
They rigged your car with bombs
And tried to run you off the road
Too often to remember.
You were a mercenary in Latin America
And a POW in Korea,
And your fellow warriors and captives
Always seemed to want to kill you
Over some grudge, as did, for that matter,
A surprising number of your college football chums.
You golfed, sailed, skied, rode horses, flew planes,
And spoke fluent Armenian,
And you always made time to join Peggy
For Toby's parent-teacher conferences.
In short, a total stud—if not exactly
Beloved by your peers. And I don't care
If it wasn't *you*-you who did all that.
You made me—middle-school me—
Believe it was you, one hundred ninety-four
Sunday nights at ten
And endlessly in reruns,
Way after the late news,
While my dad snored in rhythm
To the crackle of a TV set.

Mike Connors, 91, Star Sleuth of 'Mannix'
(January 28, 2017)

IV

Sports

They could have named a lot of things for you:
A street, a stand, a brand of cigarettes,
A shade of orange, or a state of mind.
Instead, your "Cruyff" lives in a trick, a feint,
A physical maneuver built to fool,
A gasp, a thrill, a YouTube clip that still
Leaves kids grown up on *FIFA* tantalized:

In Dortmund, World Cup number ten, first half,
Nil-nil, the right fullback for Sweden tight
On your left hip, you use an arm to make
Some space, to swing your right leg at the ball,
Intending, all the world assumes, to cross,
And then—a blink!—you tap the ball instead,
A nudge toward your *left* foot, and sprint away,
The ball expectant at your charging toes,
The poor Swede left to stare at empty air,
Just one more of the helpless mass for whom
Your genius bore a lashing of contempt.

Imperfect though the world may be at core,
In play, you found a golden ideal form
And paid no heed if anybody else
Could reach the aerie where you made your home.

Johann Cruyff, the High Priest of Dutch Soccer, Dies at 68
(March 24, 2016)

Millions of miles, it's gotta be,
You watched them run
And watched in minute detail,
Noting every pump of every toe,
Foot, calf, knee, quad, the click
Of every second on a stopwatch,
Timing their progress on circular paths
That nonetheless took them, and you,
On journeys you never imagined:
Forty-three years, thirty-four titles,
Thirteen gold medal ceremonies,
And your greatest deed, you reckoned,
All but one of your Olympians
Walking across a stage with her diploma,
Ready to take whatever step life allowed.
The race is to the swift, no doubt,
But it is also to the durable and sure.

Ed Temple Dies at 89; Coached 40 Olympians
(September 24, 2016)

Up there,
The foot in height
You ceded
To your brother
Erased,
You could see it clear,
As if you were alone,
Practicing, as you liked to:
The hoop.
And so you shot it:
Good.
The jumper,
Invented.

No matter that you never topped
Five-ten, that coaches
Could mistake a stroke of inspiration
For abomination
And sit you down
Until you gave up
"That queer shot,"
Which you never did.

Just as that first time,
You sprang and sprang
Over every earthly foe
Squared up in your face
For years, until at last

The number that you wore
Was enshrined—where else?—
High above your high school's parquet floor.

*Kenny Sailors, Who Helped Basketball Leap Forward, Dies
at 95* (February 1, 2016)

I was born a Mets fan, so doomed
By entering this vale of woe
Through the agency of two
Brokenhearted Brooklyn Dodger fans
(Were there any other kind?)
Who nearly gave up baseball
Altogether, only to be gifted
A new team and new son in the same year,
And who chose to hang on to both.

Just days before my first tears,
You, too, were born to the team,
Drafted away from Philadelphia,
Where you hit a-buck-
Twenty-eight as a rookie,
And anointed second-string catcher
On the worst team ever to play.

A lot came out of those first Mets,
Most of it not much more palatable
Than the things that came out of me,
But to spend a precious draft pick on
A catcher named Choo Choo
Who couldn't hit his weight,
Called every newsman "Bub,"
And would retire to become a Chinese cook,
That was, even for a team renowned
For terrible decisions doubled-down upon,
As notable as my toddling steps and words—

Ordinary things done endlessly since
But never with such panache as when done first.

*Choo Choo Coleman, a Catcher With the Original, Woeful
Mets* (August 16, 2016)

In retrospect, it's hard to say
Which is more amazing:
That there was a time when Jews
Dominated the basketball court
Or that there was a time when Jews
Named their children Adolph.
And yet there you were: Both.

Dolph Schayes, NBA Star, Dies at 87
(December 11, 2015)

You didn't like the nickname. Fine:
Your life; your body; your choice.
But, dude: You hit .270
With thirty-three homers in ten years:
Would you rather have been known as No *Hit*?

Walt Williams, 72, Player Known as No Neck
(January 28, 2016)

The one who first snapped his fingers,
The one who first sweetened her tea,
The pioneers of sleep masks, bicycle clips, warrior pose:
Their names are lost, even as their eurekas
Live with us daily, almost subliminal,
So one with the world that the world
Seems to have bloomed with them
Already fully formed. And yet
Someone had to do them before anyone else,
And you picked yourself a hell of a stage
To reveal something now obvious to us all:
1960, California, the Olympic downhill,
In air so cold the scoreboard froze,
You did what every skier since has done:
You tucked—knees bent, back flattened,
The air carved by your descent
Rushing past instead of pushing against you.
"*L'oeuf*," you called your stance: "the egg."
Later, you helped build a ski resort
And lent your name to a sunglass manufacturer,
And those deeds attached themselves to you,
Though your most lasting inspiration never did.
The insight that you had,
And the conviction to see it through—
A permanent mark on the world—
Would stay anonymous.
You saw a thing that should have always been
And turned a what-if into ever-was.

*Jean Vuarnet, a Downhill Innovator Who Won Olympic
Gold, Dies at 83* (January 4, 2017)

V

Political Suite

1

We're talking financial
Rather than moral,
I get it,
But thanks just the same, pal.
And how convenient for you to split
Just before the rest of us reaped
The whirlwind you helped whip up.

*Stephen Bollenbach, 74, Helped Trump Ward Off
Bankruptcy* (October 17, 2016)

2

Scrupulous,
Diligent,
Thorough,
A pioneer,
First woman
In the post,
You left us
On the eve
Of the day
A few thousand votes
Put in the office
You tirelessly
Served

A madman
You'd sharpen
Every pencil
On your desk
To bring to heel.
Adieu,
And lucky you.

*Janet Reno, First Woman to Serve As Attorney General,
Dies at 78* (November 8, 2016)

3

Sixty-two million
Nine hundred eighty-four thousand
Eight hundred twenty-five:
That's how many shots to the foot it takes
For a country to bleed itself to death.

*Trump Triumphs: Outsider Mogul Captures the
Presidency, Stunning Clinton in Battleground States*
(November 9, 2016)

VI

Noted in Passing

As a boy, I daydreamed scythes,
In the back of my dad's latest Buick,
riding highways, wielding
A long, curved blade
On an infinite handle
Reaching the horizon,
Slicing trees, utility poles,
Fence posts, stanchions of billboards,
Houses, small towns, anything,
Really, I'd a whim to,
Retracting or lifting it,
Sparing some object
Or other that, I don't know,
Pleased me at the moment.

Death also carries a scythe,
The better to grimly reap us,
One by one, our dates with doom
The weeding of a plot.
But Death's scythe adjusts, too,
And is swung
Sometimes in huge swaths—
Disasters, plagues, wars, accidents,
Or days when, if only
Because it can, it takes whomever:
A Serbian general; a prima ballerina;
A Salvadoran president; a court reporter;
An editor; a lawyer; a prisoner of war;
The author of *Georgy Girl*.

In life, they stood in fields
Of their own choosing or making,
Born at different times, in different lands,
Discreet from one another,
Ignorant of one another's works,
Growing toward the light, or not,
Creating, or not, destroying, or not,
And falling, by sheer happenstance,
Of disparate causes, foreseen or not,
On more or less the same day—
Coincidence set now in ink.

There is no thread, no *why*:
They reached the line
Between time lived
And time not
And crossed it,
Sliced down in one fell stroke
Or whittled away over weakening months,
Leaving, where once they stood firm,
The words and acts and echoes of their having been.

My blade never vanquished a thing,
Just the idea of it; Death's avails over bodies,
But the works and impressions
Those bodies created persist.
Every tree I ever lopped was left
Exactly as it had been,
Just as these lives, though ended, carry on
In the echoes and the annals of their deeds.

Margaret Forster, Author of 'Georgy Girl' and More, Dies at 77

Zdravko Tolimir, 67, General Tied to Massacre

Arnold Lubasch, 83, Covered Crime and Courts for Decades

Paul Aiken, 56, Leader of Authors Guild

Edgar Whitcomb, 98, P.O.W. and Governor

Violette Verdy, Ballerina with Flair and 'Theatrical Alchemy,' Dies at 82

Francisco Flores, 56, Salvadoran Leader

David G. Hartwell, 74; Edited Sci-Fi Books

(February 10, 2016)

One hundred fifty thousand times,
From 1930 to 2015,
On homemade gear on the family farm,
A sentinel untumbled as Gibraltar,
Unrelenting as a South Fork gale,
You took the weather,
Reporting your findings as you had learned—
On a hundred-year-old government form,
With carbon paper backup and
A call on a rotary phone.
Annually, on December 31st,
You allowed yourself a toot—
A blast from an antique cannon
That scared the chickens into a new year.
Death, illness, disaster, or (least of all) terrible
Weather: You simply never failed.
When you went to New Zealand, you appointed
A surrogate; when your wife died,
You noted the conditions at her passing. Sisyphus
Would admire your application (not to mention
Envy you your relatively cushy gig).
Perseverance, duty, keeping your word—
Call it what you may, it was heroic.
Time and tide may not wait for anyone
But you gave the bastards a hell of a fight.

Richard G. Hendrickson, 103, Dies; Recorded the Weather for 85 Years (January 18, 2016)

Pete Gray (Google him) played for St. Louis,
Seventy-seven games in left, with no right arm.

The baker in *Moonstruck,* wrist hacked in a slicer,
Enjoyed a good business. And James Hook's command

Was, likely, only enhanced by that crocodile.
But canon law requires two hands

To celebrate mass, and so
You never see a one-armed priest.

By your own account, you gave no thought
To serving on an altar, though as a boy

They once let you kiss the right arm,
The one you lacked, of St. Francis Xavier.

You hoped, instead, to grace the legitimate stage,
Despite the unmasked jibes of casting agents.

When those doors closed, you joined the Jesuits
And spent life serving other amputees, teaching them

To write, bake, and, yes, act. At sixty-six,
At last, a calling, and you had to petition

Rome to ordain you, which, *mirabile dictu,*
Someone had the common sense to do.

As if there was a God who couldn't hear
The sound of one hand clasped in prayer.

Rev. Rick Curry, 72, Dies; A Minister Via Stagecraft
(December 22, 2015)

Until you chose it
From the top row
Of the keyboard,
It was so obscure
It didn't have a name.

It's eight hundred years old,
And people have tried to call it
'Arobase,' 'arroba,'
'Aspersand,' 'amperat,'
'Snail,' 'meow sign,'
Even 'strudel.'
None took.

So, there it sat,
Hovering above the '2,'
Useful for invoices only,
Ignominious.

And then a common sign,
Something transparent
That can find just one person,
Was needed and—
Eureka!—just like that
A world's fingertips
Became accustomed to a key
We all now know as 'at.'

Because sometimes the biggest shift
Starts with a single digit.

*Raymond Tomlinson Is Dead at 74; He Put the @ in Email
Addresses* (March 8, 2016)

So many terms of art—
'Box pleat,' 'perfect roll,'
'Button tab,' 'hanger loop,'
'Color fusing,' 'candy stripe,'
'Tartan,' 'Madras.'

To the untrained eye
A shirt is a shirt is a shirt.
But to those born
To a pair of jobbers—
A collar man and a buttonholer—
Every nuance has a meaning,
Every stitch and seam its designation.

Even the family name—
Gantmacher—was tailored
To suit a new fashion:
Gant; Gant of New Haven,
Makers of Ivy League shirts,

In fact, and why not:
Give the world a thing
As common as 'button-down'
And you can call yourself
Whatever fits.

Elliot Gant, 89, Shirt Maker Who Perfected Button-Down
(March 20, 2016)

No one wiping
Their mouth
Afterward
Cares if there
Wasn't anyone
Named Mac
Or that the general
Was, in fact,
A brute.
The flavor
Is the point,
The reliable flavor,
And you both
Had the knack
For finding it and,
Yes, giving it a name.

Michael James Delligatti, 98, Creator of the Big Mac and Its 'Special Sauce' (December 1, 2016)

Peng Chang-kuei, Chef Who Created General Tso's Chicken, Is Dead at 98 (December 3, 2016)

For decades, people made their way
To deepest Alabama
In search of some thing
They'd lost
Or to get a deal
On something
Someone else did.
And you so loved
The human face
Of the work, the meeting
And getting-to-know,
That you hung around
Two decades
After you sold
The business off,
Just for sociability.
You made money, yes,
But you made friends,
Getting to know people
Even more of a thrill
Than rifling through
The lives
Packed into
Those thousands
Of suitcases
That fell
Into your hands.

Doyle Owens, 85, Unclaimed Baggage Founder
(December 12, 2016)

Of all that
Can be said
Of one
Who's gone,
The most
Bittersweet
Might be:
He died
Doing what
He loved.

Douglas Tompkins, 72, Founder of North Face, Dies in Kayak Accident (December 9, 2015)

In the yin and yang of things,
The up and down, the give and take,
You did your bit.
Many's the time I battled
With your most famous inspiration
And came away trembling,
Only to be restored the following day
By the next-most-famous thing you made.

Do your worst, red cup full of booze,
I've got black coffee,
Beneath the nipple of this plastic lid
To ease me back to par.

Robert L. Hulseman, 84, Solo Cup Inventor and Co-Creator of 'Nurturing' Traveler Lid (December 31, 2016)

There are very few people in this world without
Whom the rest of us couldn't make it through the day,
But the man who sold two hundred million
Hourglass-shaped espresso pots and even had his ashes
Buried in one: He's among them.
Dottore: A doppio to your honor.

*Renato Bialetti, Italian Marketer, Dies at 93; He Elevated a
Coffee Maker to an Emblem* (February 21, 2016)

None was Everest, true,
But none had been summited, either,
And so you took them on:
The Hidden Peak in Pakistan,
Mount Vinson in Antarctica,
And Doomsday Mountain in the Himalayas.
You planned, calculated, coached,
And sometimes didn't make it to the top
Even as your teammates did.
You weren't fazed: "The mountains
Don't care who you are." Not even the one
At the bottom of the world,
Some fifteen thousand-plus feet tall
And named for you, a piece
Of the horizon all your own: Clinch Peak.

Nicholas Clinch, 85, Dies; Took on Unclimbed Peaks
(June 24, 2016)

It's clear, years on, that it was fate:
Mom and dad eloped, after all,
And you came into the world
In the back of a Pierce-Arrow, born in transit
And into privilege. When the marriage died,
Mom made a new match the next day,
Became a Lady, in fact. But you
Felt shut inside a cage, even if
It moved around the world in luxury.
At eight, the final straw: in the dead
Of winter: Bermuda: a Christmas
With no snow. And so you slipped
Onto a boat set for New York, and when
Shore was out of sight, declared
Yourself to the captain, announcing
You were hungry. They fed you
And radioed that you were safe.
And when you hit Manhattan,
Your grandma was at the pier
With a gaggle of press men
Who compared you in one breath
To Huck Finn and Little Lord Fauntleroy.
For the rest of your life
You lived inside the lines:
Marine Corps, Yale, Harvard Law;
White shoe law firm, museum trust;
A marriage of nearly seventy years;
Kids, grandkids, great-grandkids;
You even helped reintroduce
Wolves to the Yellowstone ecosphere,

A final note of wildness, a trace
Of the boy who set off to sea alone.

Carroll L. Wainwright Jr., Estate Lawyer, 90, Dies; Stowed Away to Fame (October 2, 2016)

Nine days, eight nights;
Rain, fog, cold, flies, bears;
No shoes, no pants, no map;
On a mountain in Maine, alone;
A whole world waiting for word of you.

You remembered your scout training.
You brushed off fear, hunger, pain, hallucinations.
You wandered thirty-five miles.
You stumbled on telephone lines and followed them.

Sixteen pounds lighter,
Bled mercilessly by bugs,
Scratched, sunburnt, frightened, resolute,
You found a cabin, hollered,
And were saved.

You were twelve years old.

After wife, kids, military career,
And a memoir every Mainer read in school,
You had one wish: "My ashes
Are going over Mount Katahdin."

Seventy-eight years it waited.
It would have you in the end.

*Donn Fendler, 90, Dies; Became Lost for Days in Maine's
Wilds as Boy* (October 12, 2016)

Have a thought for the billionaire duke.
With his acres of Mayfair and Belgravia,
And his thirty-five square mile garden,
And his forebear who took up with the Normans.

Have a thought for the billionaire duke,
With his wife and her ancestor czars,
And his godsons in line to the throne,
And his knack for crashing Rollers and Jags.

Have a thought for the billionaire duke,
With his tyrant nanny and distant parents,
And his rejection from Eton, and his failed sports
    career,
And his nervous breakdowns, and his spells of
    depression,

And his workaholism and devotion to duty,
And his philanthropy, and his efforts for veterans,
And his heart attack at sixty-four,
And his word that gold isn't always a blessing.

"I would rather not have been born wealthy," he said,
And "I can't sell it. It doesn't belong to me," he said,
And "I'd rather be Joe Bloggs," he said.
Have a thought for the billionaire duke.

Gerald Grosvenor, 64, a Billionaire Duke
(August 19, 2016)

The teacher couldn't stand the way the 'R's
Stuck in your throat: "Not French enough," she said.
She shoved a pencil straight into your mouth
And hectored you to get it right. And so
You did what any proud Greek-speaker would:
You bit it—lead, paint, splinters, everything—
And spat it out, and with it all the ways
They made kids learn to speak a foreign tongue.
It took you years, but finally you stood
Before your classes, coaxing out of them
A crayon box of words you didn't speak—
Español, Deutsch, Nihongo, and Français—
With actor's polish, guile, ingenious games
So useful that the President himself
Appointed you to steer a country's schools
Toward teaching languages with warmth, not pain.
That pencil that you chomped defiantly
Would write a new script for a nation's young.

John Rassias, 90; Foreign Language Expert
(December 7, 2015)

Nobody likes a busybody,
A know-it-all, a scold.
But a kind word of advice,
A gentle warning, a note
Of friendly caution:
You can feel real gratitude
For a stranger who,
Time and again, seems only
Concerned with other people's welfare.
Cheers, mate!

Phil Sayer, 62, Voice Advising to 'Mind the Gap' in London (April 17, 2016)

For a century,
Disembodied voices
Have lived among us:
Souls transported
Through ether
Into our homes,
Workspaces,
Earbuds, cars.

Some are daily presences
More familiar than kin—
Comforts, stalwarts, chums,
Even if we don't know
What they look like
Much less
What they *are* like.
Blind friendship;
Bonds without bodies.

But what more proof
Of corporeality
Than sudden death?
And what deeper proof
Of how little we know
Than to learn that one such voice,
So timely and reliable and true,
Sang also in a choir,
A piece of a great whole,
And spent days steering teens
In addiction and depression counseling?

That voice bespoke
A throat, a pair of lungs,
A consciousness, a heart,
And, one-to-many, many-to-one,
One-to-one, carried words
Of warning, comfort, wisdom, hope, and care
Through airways—intimate or vast—
To ears in search of
Data, consolation,
Or the simple joy of song,
And though it is now silent
I hear it forever anew.

Craig Windham, NPR News Voice, 66
(March 3, 2016)

Twinship—
One in two; two, one—
Defined you, surely,
Just as it kept you down:
That five-hour gap between
Your brother and you
Meant you'd always be
Second to him in line.

Actually, worse:
In a culture bent
On raw misogyny,
A woman couldn't
Compete at all,
Let alone take silver.

But you had access to a pulpit
And used it to campaign
For fair play for your sisters,
Appearing unscarved in public,
Living the freedom you truly believed.

Your birthright, though,
Could also be a sword,
And you swung it to command
Respect, even in exile,
Despite your family's crimes,
atrocities far worse than veils.

Elegant, progressive,
Superior, mean,
You railed against the chador
Wearing mink,
Fought for the trampled
While defending a tyrant,
Championed a nation's poor
From a chateau in Juan-les-Pins.

You weren't just a twin:
You were a Janus.

Ashraf Pahlavi, 96, Twin Sister of Iran's Last Shah
(January 9, 2016)

The Alous I knew,
The Karamazovs,
The Corleones;
But a third Castro?
That was news.

Eldest, a landowner
Who saw his acres
Scarfed up by revolution,
A lifelong campesino
Whose little brothers
Tilted at the world.

No Fredo, no Alyosha, no Jesús,
Content to watch history pass
From the vantage of a farmhouse porch.

Ramón Castro, 91, Brother to Revolutionaries
(February 25, 2016)

"There was nothing but trouble," you said,
"From the minute that crown touched my head."
You wanted to study music
In New York, and on a side trip
To Atlantic City wound up
Being named Miss America,
A Miss America who refused
To wear swimsuits during her reign.
"I'm an opera singer," you said,
"Not a pin-up girl!," which so incensed
The sponsors that they set up
Their own pageant: Miss USA.

You didn't care. The noise
Around your stance helped throw
A light on social justice—
Your true great passion.
You swelled the crowds at
The Rosenbergs' execution,
Civil Rights marches, Ban-the-Bomb rallies.
"I'm a Southern girl," you said,
"But I'm a thinking girl,"
Which was how your brain and heart
Told the rest of your body who was boss.

*Yolande Betbeze Fox, 87, Miss America Who Refused to
Tour in Bathing Suits* (February 26, 2016)

The commitment you made at sixteen
Demanded you'd have no kids,
And you held to that path:
Celibate, pious, true.
But you were impish
And, when young,
Slightly wicked,
And then, almost famously
(As much as faith allowed),
Active and worldly and iconic,
Ambassador for a culture that,
As if by design,
Will die away,
Breeding livestock,
Tending a garden,
Cooking, singing, writing,
And welcoming the world
To the community
That shrunk around you
Without ever once
Diminishing your spirit.

Sister Frances Ann Carr, 89, One of the Last Three Shakers
(January 5, 2017)

We think it all began
With a particle
Exploding into
Everything,
So why shouldn't
The ideal male body
Be perfectly petite
And belong to a man
Whose life motto
Was just as compact?
"As it is,"
You always said,
And you lived it,
Galaxies of calm—
And millions of push-ups—
Describing your arc.

*Manohar Aich, 103, Who Won Mr. Universe Title at
4-Foot-11* (June 13, 2016)

At the time—and even more today—
It seemed absurd to eighty-six
An astronaut because of a divorce.
But such was the culture in '65
That they bounced you, and home you went
To Vermont and not one,
Not two, not three, not four, but *five*
New wives, and a medical career
And charges of missing narcotics
And children inappropriately touched.
There was damage in you, clearly,
And no way, in those times,
For NASA, with its slide rules and square heads,
To see someone like you or to help you heal.

Duane Graveline, Forced Out as Astronaut, Dies at 85
(September 18, 2016)

Your dad made shoes,
And your brother made shoes,
And all your daughters
Make shoes to this day,
And you were a shoeman, too,
Of course: sixty-three years,
Three classic designs,
Two hundred fifty million pairs out the door,
Natty, mustachioed, spry,
With an eye for a cut,
A feel for the price,
And the art
To make your oldest girl
Chief creative officer
Of the firm that bears her name.
Beautifully polished
And neatly done.

Stanley Silverstein, 91; Co-founded Nina Footwear
(October 31, 2016)

'A New York dame,'
And what a thing to be,
The talk of uptown
Or envy of down,
Inspiration for one song
Or thousands of printed words,
Flickering
A few brilliant moments
On celluloid
Or shining as a lodestar,
Ever-fixèd, pointing toward
The Upper West Side.

Amid the city's grid lines and ado,
Your arcs surely crossed,
And it pleases me to think
However rude the ruckus,
Whatever the bustle,
Whether introduced or not,
You caught each other's eye,
Even if for a second,
And saw yourselves
Gazing back
Appreciatively.

*Holly Woodlawn, Transgender Star of Underground Films,
Is Dead at 69*

*Janet Wolfe, 101, a Gleeful Gadabout Who Got the Town
Talking, Is Dead*

(December 8, 2015)

A simpleton like me, head full
Of Bond and Bourne and Le Carré,
Can feel roused to expect fireworks
At reading such a thrilling word as "spy,"
And feel a pinch of disappointment
When encountering mere stupendous
Courage in workaday guise.
And so it is the cool light of the real,
The truth of life, can seem mundane, when clearly
Life itself, alone, is filled with twists
And traps and perils, and those confronted
With its most intense episodes—
Nazis maneuvering around Sicily;
Brainwashing at the hands of Mao's Reds—
Are stone remarkable without the need
For histrionics concocted by dreamers
(Sedentary men, for the most part)
Who rarely leave the comfort of their dens.

Harriet Mills, Scholar Accused of Spying, 95
(April 2, 2016)

Doris Bohrer, 93, Spy for Allies In Italy During World War II (August 23, 2016)

"Why do you wear that stuff?"
She asked, and you could have answered,
"I sell rarities at high prices and need to look the part,"
Or, "I was a dancer and still care for form,"
Or, "My British parents raised me to be proper,"
Or, "I've quit booze, and it's a sign of self-respect."

But the woman doing the asking
Was Mother Teresa, for whom you'd come
Half around the world to work,
And, for once, you said nothing
And accepted the lesson.

At auctions, you sold beauty,
Goading the mob
Into spending yet more,
Famous for
Your wit and wardrobe,
Until the day
You up and left
To feed, inoculate, and succor
Those with nothing,
Putting your silver tongue
In the service of a golden heart,
Slightly tarnished,
You'd be first to admit,
But no less rare
Or valuable
For that.

*Lorna Kelly, Who Left the Rostrum at Sotheby's to Help
the Poor, Dies at 70* (June 22, 2016)

In 1969, three people on the planet *maybe*
Could transplant a beating heart
Into a living human,
And two of them lived in Texas
And hated each other's guts.

They'd been mentor and trainee,
Friends, partners. But the younger
Leapt ahead and put an artificial ticker
Into a man who lived but four more days.

Questions of patents, ethics, glory-seeking,
And unbecoming zeal arose,
And for nearly forty years
The two didn't speak; the spat
Even made the cover of *Life*.

A year before the elder died,
Though, the briefest thaw:
A handshake, a medal, some kind words,
A pair of hardheaded hotshots
Laying down their scalpels
And sharing with one another
At last—what else?—their hearts.

*Dr. Denton Cooley, Heart Surgery Pioneer Who Set Off a
40-Year-Feud, Dies at 96* (November 19, 2016)

Ten thousand doses, or
Forty-three pills a day
For the two hundred twenty-eight days
Of 1977 that he lived.

Diabetes, glaucoma, migraines, hypertension,
Arrhythmia, insomnia, allergies, adrenal deficiency,
And, of course, megacolon—
The chronic constipation those pills caused
And which he strained so mightily against
He broke his own heart dead one sorry night.

"I cared too much," you told them
When they took your license away.
In fact, you cared so much you wrote
A book about him and mounted
A traveling show that included
An empty Dilaudid bottle
With his name on it.

He lived to forty-two; you made eighty-eight.
And the only reason I
Know who you are
Is, like those evil pricks
Remembered in history books
By all three of their names,
You killed somebody
Greater than yourself.

George Nichopolous, 88 Dies; Elvis Presley's Doctor
(February 27, 2016)

A baby blue Bel Air;
A moon; an empty road;
A car in a blind, idling, pouncing;
A chase; shotgun blasts;
A standoff: The bastard
In the road, firing back,
Screaming, and, from your belly,
Lying in the grass,
You, putting one through his chin.

The goat, Trujillo, finally dead.

Thirty years he ravaged a country—
Its money, its daughters, its land—
Until you and a band of thirteen
Vowed to see it end.
And so you did.

His loyalists hunted you for years—
Winged you once, in fact—
But you were on the side of history
And down to earth about it: Each year
On the day you struck the tyrant down,
You put on the very same brown shoes
You wore that night you tore your nation free.
"The only way to get rid of him
Was to kill him," you explained,
Both feet planted firmly on the ground.

Antonio Imbert Barrera, 95, Dictator's Killer, Dies
(June 8, 2016)

The deaths you cause
Can outweigh the life you live.

One of you killed for hate:
A man alone, a minister
Come from Boston to Alabama
To swell a march and foster progress
Only to be jumped by an ugly little mob
And have his skull crushed,
For which crime you were fingered
Straightaway, and then acquitted
In a courtroom any self-respecting kangaroo
Would be ashamed to have named for it.

One of you killed for spite:
Drunk and out of work, pissed off at a girl,
You bought a gallon of gas
And lit a fire at the door to Happy Land,
The nightclub where she worked,
The *only* door, a shocked world learned,
After eighty-seven bodies were recovered,
For each of which you got one whole life term.

And you? You did nothing
But hit your mark, say your lines,
And use the prop gun you'd been handed,
Just as you'd been told to,
Not knowing a shell
Was still inside, that shrapnel
Would pierce another actor's guts,
And that he'd die for real after dying for play.

Brandon Lee was twenty-eight, and no one blamed you
Or brought you to trial,
But you testified all the same: "I don't think,"
You said, "You ever get over something like that."

No, not with an ounce of human decency,
An ounce not granted everyone, you don't.

Namon O'Neal Hoggle, 81, Is Dead; Acquitted in a Civil Rights Killing (September 7, 2016)

Julio Gonzalez, Arsonist Who Killed 87 at a New York Club in 1990, Dies at 61 (September 15, 2016)

Michael Massee, 64, Actor Haunted by Gun Accident (October 30, 2016)

VII

In the Newsroom

Sometimes I just wanna give
The headline writer such a zetz.

Dude's boat was brand new to him;
Dude's crew didn't know each other;
Dude was mocked for being Mexican by the Brits;
Dude—and all other hands—survived a capsizing;
Dude was a *washing machine salesman*, for the love of
    Mike.
And in one hundred thirty-three days and thirteen
    hours
All dude did was sail around the world—
Twenty-seven thousand miles—
A full two days faster than
The professional crews
He was racing against,

And forty years later, some wiseacre desk jockey in
    New York
Tops a brilliant account of the man and his feat
With the word, maybe meant as a compliment,
    "casual."

Twenty-seven thousand fucking miles:
Casual my ass.

*Ramón Carlín, Casual Sailor Who Won a Round-the-
World Race, Dies at 92* (May 11, 2016)

And then there are the days
When you just know
The universe —
Or
At least
The obit editor —
Is winking. To wit:

A televangelist and a pioneer
In feminist public radio
Show up, one
Atop
The other,
Even though
They died
A week apart.

I get how
These things happen:
Vagaries of reporting,
Editing, news holes,
Unforeseen events.

But I also like to think
That God —
Or that obit editor —
Is having
A laugh
And that
We'll never know

In this life
Whom it's on.

Janice Crouch Dies at 78; Led Religious Network

Nanette Raione, 73, Feminist Radio Creator

(June 2, 2016)

'Asshole.'
The word you're looking for
But can't bring yourself
To publish is
'Asshole.'

Sam Bell, 88, an Exacting Mentor of Runners
(June 28, 2016)

Edward Davis, 'World's Grumpiest Boss,' Dies at 85
(September 26, 2016)

VIII

The Personals

I had no appetite, then
Or now, for your Prince.
Ours was a Ronzoni house
And would not budge,
And of such prejudices
Whole lives are built.

But ours was also a family
Of Anthonys,
After my great-grandfather,
Abandoned, per our legend,
By a teenage mom
In a bureau drawer
In Pagani, near Pompeii,
And rescued by a neighbor
Who shipped him off
Alone, a few years later,
To America.

Big Tony Pariso, as I knew him,
Who ran a junkyard in Brooklyn
And had an Anthony of his own—
Even bigger—who *also* had an Anthony.
There was a cousin Anthony in Maryland,
And at least a half-dozen among us
Whose various names
Bore an Anthony in the middle,
Including me.
And I, in my turn,
Named an Anthony as well.

So, it wasn't the brand of spaghetti
That warmed me to you—
And we called it macaroni, anyhow,
No matter the shape.
No, it was that holler
Out the window—
"*Anthony!*
Anthony!"—
That marked you,
Nameless though you were,
As my blood.

Mary Fiumara, 88, Mother in a Spaghetti Ad
(February 5, 2016)

Not long after I was born—
I mean, like, hours—
My father left the maternity ward
And came back from your place,
Already an institution
Though barely a decade old,
With a piece of your signature dish
Which my mother no doubt ate
In bliss and gratitude
While I got ... formula.

In time, I would have my fill
Of your specialty (and would happily
Gobble some up right now),
But that slice I was denied
Has transformed from family anecdote
To beguiling intimation
Of some central truths of life:
Some sup on cheesecake;
Some get a bottle full of pap;
And sometimes a parent deserves to be spoilt
And a child made to wait for a sweet reward.

*Walter Rosen, 81, Steward of Junior's, a New York
Cheesecake Benchmark* (April 15, 2016)

I never saw you play; there was no need.
From the time I was aware
There was such a thing as baseball,
I heard your name,
Sometimes with bitterness,
Sometimes with laughter
Riddled with bitterness,
But never blithely,
Never neutrally, and never, *ever*
Forgiven or forgotten.
I'm not going to say
My dad died hating you—
It wasn't his nature—
But the mention of you
Could dim his mood decades on.
He was twenty-two when it happened;
You, twenty-five.
Bottom of the ninth, one out,
The Bums up two,
You threw one high and in,
And *crack*: the bat on the ball;
The voice on the radio;
The hearts of all Brooklyn;
The story of the season;
The annal of your life, and my dad's.
"A guy commits murder," you said,
"And he gets pardoned
After twenty years."
Not you. You kept playing,
Married, had kids,
Did good works, won game shows,

Sat for interviews, and passed at ninety —
A full and decent life,
And they *never* let it go.
My dad, for one, who spoke
Of broken-hearted friends and kin;
Of the ghost of Ebbets Field,
Wandering apartments
Built after the Dodgers
Lit out for the coast,
Wailing in the night;
Of *almost* stopping by a bank
Where you were signing autographs
To remind you what had happened
(As if you'd ever forgotten),
Haunted by a ballgame
Decades after the fact.
That was his lot —
His and yours, to be fair,
For though you didn't know him,
He was bound to you
By an accident of physics, fate,
And the elixir of fandom,
Which can feed briars and thorns
In otherwise placid fields,
Even the one in my head,
Where you never once set foot.

*Ralph Branca, 1926-2016: Dodgers Pitcher Who Gave Up
'Shot Heard Round the World'* (November 24, 2016)

The last time I saw you,
Outside Movie Madness
On a spring afternoon
In the company of your husband,
A college beau with whom you'd reconnected,
You were as I'll always remember you:
Smiling, laughing, sweet,
Asking what I'd seen,
What I was writing.

I was always running into you like that—
Trader Joe's, Coffee Time,
The occasional screening or party—
And you couldn't have been more dear, or,
For want of a female equivalent, avuncular:
Aunt Katherine, who adopted me
The moment I rolled into Oregon
And was kind to me and my work
In ways I've never fully been myself.

That fond aura you bore in the world
Was hard to reconcile with your art,
So full of blood and hurt and gross,
A shadowland of dark and weird ....
A mystery that the words
That conjured all of that
Came from a soul so homey, down to earth.

But, of course, your empathy for one
Was empathy for all, and the way
You spoke of freaks and villains
And, when I best knew you, boxers—
Even Iron Mike Tyson, who, you swore,
Was absolutely right to chomp an ear
And defend himself—
Was another aspect
Of your native need
To check up on the world.

That was your heart in action:
Vision beneath the obvious,
Finding the human core,
Making us know its taste.
And so, weeks after that last encounter,
When the shock of your passing
Rippled the community you made,
I recognized with shame
That I didn't ask enough
After *you*, that something in me
Left me dumb and blind,
That I didn't see beneath *your* skin,
Where, despite the sun and grins
And niceties, something lurked
That would take you, soon and fast.

And so, this adieu, which is also a 'thanks,'
Is, as well, an 'I'm sorry,'
For being trapped inside myself,
For not asking questions,
For not seeing the you in you,
For having been unable to connect
As I now wish I had
With a heart so rare and dear and true.

Katherine Dunn, Author of the Offbeat and Inventive 'Geek Love,' Dies at 70 (May 16, 2016)

Valedictory

At twenty-four, a chipper
Suburban wife and mom;
At thirty-three, a career girl
Making her way alone;
At forty-three, a stoic
Too cold to succor a suicidal son;

And informing them all: wit, talent,
Beauty, grace, real dancing chops,
And, chiefly, perhaps,
The determination
To not let any man—
Not your TV or film spouses
Or your three real-world ones—
Tell you what you could
Or could not do,

Not you, who survived
A sorrowful childhood,
The death of a son,
Your own alcoholism,
And everything Hollywood,
In its infinite piggery,
Could throw at you,

Not you, whose laugh and smile
Had, per the song,
Transformative powers,
Who trafficked in pep or sex
Or steel as the moment required,
And who, when you chose to

Toss your tam o'shanter in joy,
Could do so in such a way
That it never fell back to earth,
Not even to this day.

*Mary Tyler Moore, 1936-2017: Television's Spunky
Modern Woman Incarnate* (January 26, 2017)

APPENDIX 1
Obit

Toward the end of the year-plus during which I gathered the materials for this book, I experienced one of those unpredictable coincidences of life: In my physical postal mailbox, I received a screening copy of the documentary *Obit* by Vanessa Gould, a portrait of life at *The New York Times* obituary desk and clippings morgue.

For years, I had read and appreciated the work of such *NYT* staff writers as Margalit Fox, William Grimes, William McDonald, and Bruce Weber. Now here they were on my TV, along with their editors and colleagues, selecting subjects, doing research, writing against deadlines, and generally engaged in the sorts of decisions, revisions, and (sigh) corrections that were deeply familiar to me as a newscritter of decades tenure.

I was impressed with the moviemaking, with the personalities, with the portrait of work. And what was even more exciting was that I was at that very moment engaged in this specific project involving the specific creations of these obituarists, meaning that three of the circles of the Venn Diagram of my life—journalist, film critic, and poet—met in one informative and enjoyable movie.

As a critic and connoisseur of death notices, I heartily recommend *Obit*.

And as a reader of newspapers and the composer of these poems, I am deeply grateful to the people who wrote the obituaries on which they are based.

Firstly, the full-time obituarists, each of whom was responsible for several of the articles that I used as prompts for my poems: Margalit Fox, Anita Gates, William Grimes, Robert Lipsyte, William McDonald, Robert D. McFadden, Sam Roberts, Eli Rosenberg, Richard Sandomir, Daniel E. Slotnik, and Bruce Weber. I deeply appreciate and recognize their prose, research, doggedness, and thoroughness—their professionalism, in a word.

Another group of writers composed only one or two of the obits that I used as starting points, but, chosen by their editors for their special knowledge of a language, a place, or a subject matter, they were equally invaluable: Lawrence K. Altman, Geeta Anand, Dave Anderson, Jess Bidgood, Lou Cannon, Sewell Chan, Niraj Chokshi, Andrew Das, Randi Hutter Epstein, Richard Goldstein, Eric Grode, Carl Hulse, Dave Itzkoff, Jonathan Kandell, Peter Keepnews, Anna Kisselgoff, Allan Kozinn, Andrew E. Kramer, Stuart Lavietes, Adam Liptak, Frank Litsky, Mike McPhate, Barry Meier, Christopher Mele, Jon Pareles,

Larry Rohter, Rick Rojas, John Schwartz, Kirk Semple, Marlise Simons, Robert Simonson, and Daniel Victor.

To each I wish meaty assignments, comfortable deadlines, cooperative interviewees, well-pleased editors, never-empty coffee mugs, and an endless string of bylines without corrections.

Dash-Thirty-Dash, yo.

APPENDIX 2
They, Too, Were Here
(a curated selection of other notable deaths recorded in
The New York Times during the composition of these poems)

*Lillian Vernon, the Creator of an Empire Built on
Monogrammed Gifts, Dies at 88* (December 15, 2015)

*Robert Stigwood, Entrepreneur of Rock And Film, Is Dead
at 81* (January 5, 2016)

*Vilmos Zsigmond, 85, Cinematographer Who Shaped
Hollywood, Dies* (January 5, 2016)

*Andre Courreges, Fashion Designer Who Redefined
Couture, Dies at 92* (January 8, 2016)

*Monte Irvin, Star Outfielder Who Lost His Prime Years to
Racism, Dies at 96* (January 13, 2016)

Alan Rickman, An Actor Known for 'Harry Potter,' Dies at 69 (January 14, 2016)

Glenn Frey, 67, Singer-Songwriter and Eagles Founding Member, Dies (January 18, 2016)

Bill Johnson, a Skier Who Reached Stunning Highs and Lows, Dies at 55 (January 23, 2016)

Marvin Minsky of M.I.T. Is Dead at 88; Early Explorer of Artificial Intelligence (January 26, 2016)

Henry Worsley, a British Adventurer Trying to Cross Antarctica, Dies at 55 (January 26, 2016)

Vincent Cianci, Beloved and Scorned As Mayor of Providence, Dies at 74 (January 29, 2016)

Artur Fischer, 96, a German Tinkerer With More Patents Than Edison, Is Dead (February 9, 2016)

Denise Matthews, 57, Singer Known as Vanity (February 17, 2016)

Angela Raiola, 55, 'Big Ang' of 'Mob Wives' Reality Show (February 19, 2016)

Fernando Cardenal, 82, Priest Who Defied a Pope (February 29, 2016)

George Kennedy Dies at 91; Hollywood's Leading Sidekick (March 1, 2016)

Clyde Lovellette, 86, One of the Early Big Men of Basketball, Is Dead (March 11, 2016)

Lawrence Van Gelder, Newsman of New York and the Times, 83 (March 12, 2016)

Ken Adam, 95, Designer for 'Dr. Strangelove' And Bond Films, Dies (March 14, 2016)

Gogi Grant, 91; Topped Elvis with 'Wayward Wind' (March 16, 2016)

Geoffrey H. Hartman, Scholar Who Saw Literary Criticism as Art, Dies at 86 (March 21 2016)

Rob Ford, Blustery Ex-Mayor of Toronto Whose Struggles Went Public, Dies at 46 (March 23, 2106)

Andrew S. Grove, Who Spurred Semiconductor Revolution, Dies at 79 (March 23, 2016)

Malik Taylor, 45, Tribe Called Quest's Phife Dawg, Dies (March 23, 2016)

Joe Garagiola, a Catcher Who Called A Better Game on TV, Is Dead at 90 (March 24, 2106)

Santiago Erevia, 69, Once Denied Medal of Honor Over Ethnicity (March 26, 2016)

Jim Harrison, 1937-2016: Author of 'Legends of the Fall' and a Man of Profound Appetites (March 28, 2016)

Gato Barbieri, Trailblazer in Latin Jazz, Is Dead at 83 (April 4, 2016)

Adrienne Corri, 84, Actress in 'A Clockwork Orange' (April 4, 2016)

Winston Moseley, Unsparing Killer of Kitty Genovese, Dies in Prison at 81 (April 5, 2016)

Joseph Medicine Crow, 102, Tribal War Chief (April 6, 2016)

Toni Grant, Psychotherapist, Dies at 73; Her Couch Was on the AM Radio Dial (April 9, 2016)

David Gest Is Dead at 62; A Celebrity of Reality TV (April 13, 2016)

Pearl Washington, 52, Dies; Starred at Syracuse (April 21, 2016)

Chyna, 46, Pro Wrestler Who Became Reality Star (April 23, 2016)

Daniel J. Berrigan, 1921-2016: Antiwar Priest Preached Peace And Defiance (May 1, 2016)

Mark Lane, Early Kennedy Assassination Conspiracy Theorist, Dies at 89 (May 13, 2016)

Morley Safer, Chronicler of Vietnam and Mainstay of '60 Minutes,' Dies at 84 (May 20, 2016)

Alan Young, 96, the Affable Owner on 'Mr. Ed' (May 21, 2016)

Mell Lazarus, Cartoonist, Dies at 89; Creator of 'Miss Peach' and 'Momma' (May 26, 2016)

Rick MacLeish, a Flyers Broad Street Bully, Dies at 66 (June 1, 2016)

Connie Kopelov, 90; Marriage Broke Barriers (June 1, 2016)

Peter Shaffer, Who Dissected Male Psyche in 'Equus' and 'Amadeus,' Dies at 90 (June 7, 2016)

Viktor Korchnoi, Chess Giant Who Fled U.S.S.R., 85 (June 7, 2016)

Gordie Howe, Tough and Durable Mr. Hockey, Dies at 88 (June 10, 2016)

Stuart Anderson, 93, Restaurateur (June 10, 2016)

Prince Be, Who Infused Rap With Mysticism, Dies at 46 (June 20, 2016)

Bernie Worrell, Funk's Master Keyboardist, Dies at 72 (June 25, 2016)

Ralph Stanley, 89, Mountain Musician Who Helped Give Rise to Bluegrass (June 25, 2016)

Michael Herr Is Dead at 76; Author of a Vietnam Classic (June 25, 2016)

Bill Cunningham, 1929-2016: A Lens on Style, Low and High, On the Street (June 26, 2016)

Goro Hawegawa, 83, Dies; Created Board Game Othello (June 27, 2016)

Pat Summitt, 1952-2016: A Coach, a Pioneer and a Most Prolific Winner (June 29, 2016)

Abner Mikva, Lawmaker, Judge and Mentor to Obama, Is Dead at 90 (July 6, 2016)

Yves Bonnefoy, 93, Pre-Eminent French Poet and Shakespeare Translator (July 6, 2016)

Carl Haas, 87, an Owner of a Formidable IndyCar Team (July 10, 2016)

Alan Vega, Punk Music Pioneer and Artist, Dies at 78
(July 18, 2016)

Nate Thurmond, 74, Dies; Battled N.B.A.'s Big Men
(July 18, 2016)

Garry Marshall, TV and Film Comedy Mastermind, Dies at 81 (July 21, 2016)

Betsy Bloomingdale, Socialite And Friend to Elite, Dies at 93 (July 22, 2016)

Forrest E. Mars Jr., 84, Candy Scion, Dies (July 28, 2016)

Jack Davis, of the Usual Gang of Idiots at Mad, Dies at 91 (July 29, 2016)

Gloria DeHaven, the Fantasy Sweetheart In Many a Movie Musical, Is Dead at 91 (August 2, 2016)

Mary Ann Madden, 83, Creator of Wordplay Contests (August 4, 2016)

Elliot Tiber, 81, Who With a Permit Unleashed Woodstock and Himself, Dies (August 8, 2016)

Glenn Yarbrough, Lyric Folk Tenor With the Limeliters, Is Dead at 86 (August 13, 2016)

Fyvush Finkel, Pillar of Yiddish Theater, Dies at 93 (August 15, 2016)

Kenny Baker, 81, Played the R2-D2 Robot in 'Star Wars' (August 15, 2016)

John McLaughlin, TV Host Who Made Combat of Punditry, Dies at 89 (August 17, 2016)

Joao Havelange, Brazilian Who Built and Ruled World Soccer, Dies at 100 (August 17, 2016)

Bobby Hutcherson, 75, Jazz Vibraphonist With Luminescent and Coolly Fluent Style (August 17, 2016)

Arthur Hiller, 'Love Story' Director And Box-Office Magnet, Dies at 92 (August 18, 2016)

Susan Baer, 65; Ran New York Area's 3 Major Airports (August 18, 2016)

Steven Hill, Who Starred on 'Law & Order,' Dies at 94 (August 24, 2016)

Jerry Heller, 75, Promoter of N.W.A and Gangsta Rap (September 5, 2016)

Phyllis Schlafly, 1924-2016: 'First Lady' of a Movement That Steered U.S. to the Right (September 6, 2016)

Hugh O'Brian, Dashing Leading Man Remembered for 'Wyatt Earp,' Dies at 91 (September 6, 2016)

Margrit Mondavi, 91, Partner in California Winery (September 6, 2016)

Vertamae Smart-Grosvenor Dies at 79; a 'Culinary Griot,' Actress and NPR Host (September 8, 2016)

W. P. Kinsella, 81, Whose Book Became 'Field of Dreams' (September 19, 2016)

Curtis Hanson, Filmmaker, Dies at 71; Won an Oscar for 'L.A. Confidential' (September 22, 2016)

Shimon Peres, an Enduring Pillar of Israel, Dies at 93 (September 29, 2016)

Richard Trentlage, 87; Wrote 'Oscar Mayer Wiener Song' (September 30, 2016)

Suzanne Mitchell, 73, Dies; Gave Cheerleading Face-Lift (October 1, 2016)

Neville Marriner, a Prolific Musician And Acclaimed Conductor, Dies at 92 (October 3, 2016)

Gordon Davidson, Artistic Director Of Mark Taper Forum, Dies at 83 (October 4, 2016)

Dario Fo, Oft-Censored Nobel Winner Who Outraged Authority, Dies at 90 (October 14, 2016)

Phil Chess, Whose Label Elevated Unknown Blues Singers, Dies at 95 (October 20, 2016)

Ted V. Mikels, Film Master of the Gory, the Buxom and the Cheesy, Dies at 87 (October 21, 2916)

Kevin Meaney, Stand-Up Comedian, Is Dead at 60 (October 24, 2016)

Tom Hayden, Civil Rights and Peace Activist Turned Lawmaker, Dies at 76 (October 25, 2016)

Bobby Vee, Teenage Pop Idol, Dies at 73; Known for 'Take Good Care of My Baby' (October 25, 2016)

Junko Tabei, Conqueror Of Everest, Is Dead at 77 (October 27, 2016)

Jack T. Chick, 92, Cartoonist Whose Tracts Preached Salvation (October 27, 2016)

Tammy Grimes, the Original 'Unsinkable Molly Brown,' Dies at 82 (November 1, 2016)

James Galanos, 92, Fashion Designer for America's Elite (November 1, 2016)

Norman Brokaw, Agent to A-Listers From Elvis to Eastwood, Dies at 89 (November 2, 2016)

Rosamond Bernier, an Elegant Art Insider Whose Lectures Dazzled, Dies at 100 (November 11, 2016)

Leon Russell, a Rock Wizard Who Mixed Soul, Country and Blues, Dies at 74 (November 14, 2016)

Mose Allison, an Influential Fount Of Jazz and Delta Blues, Dies at 89 (November 16, 2016)

William Trevor, Who Rendered the Ordinary Extraordinary, Dies at 88 (November 22, 2016)

Florence Henderson, Brady Bunch Mom, Dies at 82 (November 26, 2016)

Fidel Castro, 1926-2016: A Revolutionary Who Defied the U.S. And Held Cuba in His Thrall (November 27, 2106)

Raynoma Singleton, Early Motown Force, Dies at 79 (December 4, 2016)

Sammy Lee, Olympic Trailblazer for Asian-American Men, Dies at 96 (December 5, 2016)

Van Williams, 82, Who Played Title Role in 'The Green Hornet' (December 6, 2016)

John Glenn: 1921-2016: American Hero of the Space Age (December 9, 2016)

Shirley Hazzard, 85, Writer Who Shared Life's Cruelties (December 14, 2016)

Bishop Javier Echevarria, Leader of Opus Dei Since 1994, Dies at 84 (December 15, 2016)

Alan Thicke, 69, 'Growing Pains' Actor (December 15, 2016)

Craig Sager, 65, Sideline Reporter Whose Outfits Stole Spotlight, Dies (December 16, 2016)

China Machado, 1929-2016: A Model Who Shattered Barriers Until the End (December 20, 2016)

Fernande Grudet, 92, Dies; Ran High-Society Brothel (December 24, 2016)

George Michael, 53, Pop Superstar Who Rose to Fame in Wham!, Dies (December 26, 2016)

Haskell Wexler, 93, Dies; Distinct Cinematographer (December 28, 2016)

Vesna Vulovic, 66, Survivor of Midair Jetliner Explosion (December 29, 2016)

Allan Williams, 86, The First Manager For the Beatles, Dies (January 2, 2017)

John Berger 90, Provocative Art Critic And Author of 'Ways of Seeing,' Is Dead (January 3, 2017)

Nat Hentoff, a Writer, a Jazz Critic and Above All a Provocateur, Dies at 91 (January 9, 2017)

Om Puri, a Film Actor Who Rose With India's New Wave, Dies at 66 (January 10, 2017)

Martha Swope, Whose Photos Etched Dance and Theater History, Dies at 88 (January 13, 2017)

Nicky Scarfo, 'a Mob Boss for the 1980s,' Dies at 87 (January 18, 2017)

Miguel Ferrer, 61, Celebrated As a Film and TV Tough Guy (January 21, 2017)

William A. Hilliard, 89, Unifying Black Journalist, Dies (January 22, 2017)

Brunhilde Pomsel, Aide to Goebbels And Witness to Nazis' Fall, Dies at 106 (January 31, 2017)

ACKNOWLEDGMENTS

I'm the one who labored to bring this book into the world, but it has three mothers, without whom it would not exist at all: Eve Connell of University of Hell Press, who cheered it from the first and edited and shepherded it with care and constancy; mentor and merwoman Lidia Yuknavitch, whose workshops helped unstop the poet dormant inside the journalist lo these many years; and my beloved, Shannon Brazil, who has unfailingly encouraged, challenged, and championed me, and who made this book—and, really, everything I've written since we've met—better in every phrase. I love them all.

There's also a stepdaddy: Craig Florence of Portland's remarkable Mother Foucault's Bookshop, who gave me space and time to write, ceaseless morale boosts, and a 1:00 a.m. reading spot in his Bookseller's Ball, which made me something like the antepenultimate reader at the 2019 AWP conference. I love that guy, too.

I've previously shared some of these poems at two venues in Portland that I treasure: the original Salon

Skid Row, hosted in an off-track betting parlor by Josh Lubin; and the Salon Rouge, a magical performance space whose proprietors, my dear chums Pat Janowski and Mark Savage, have been unwavering in their friendship and advocacy.

And, since we're talking family, thanks to the Portland writing community, in particular the sub-tribes associated with Dangerous Writing, Corporeal Writing, Mother Foucault's, the Airstream Poetry Festival, and, especially, The Gong Show.

I'm grateful to the readers who offered perspective on draft versions of the manuscript: Shannon Brazil, Mo Daviau, Stevan Allred, and Mark Savage.

At University of Hell, I'm deeply appreciative of editor Eve Connell and publisher Greg Gerding. And thanks to Gigi Little, a dear friend who was on the bill the night I first shared these poems, for her gorgeous cover and design. What superb collaborators!

As ever, I'm grateful to my agent, Richard Pine, who never once questioned my intention to pursue this project. Also, as ever, my kids, Vincent, Anthony, and, especially, Paula, inspired me throughout the years of creation.

And to the dedicatees of this book—those many people who've taught, edited, copy-edited, and published me over the decades: I humbly thank you, from my deepest heart, for your time, your talents, and, chief of all, your trust.

INDEX OF SUBJECTS

AUTHOR BIO

Shawn Levy is the bestselling author of *The Castle on Sunset, Paul Newman: A Life, Rat Pack Confidential,* and other books of biography and pop culture history. A former film critic for *The Oregonian* and KGW-TV, he has written for *The New York Times, Interview, Sight and Sound, Variety, The Guardian, The Village Voice, The Black Rock Beacon,* and many, many other publications. He holds an MFA in Poetry from the University of California, Irvine and serves on the board of Operation Pitch Invasion in Portland, Oregon. (He is *not* the Shawn Levy who produces and directs *Stranger Things,* and, no, he doesn't know how to contact him.)

Visit *this* Shawn Levy at shawnlevy.com for more.

THIS BOOK IS ONE OF THE
MANY AVAILABLE FROM
UNIVERSITY OF HELL PRESS.
DO YOU HAVE THEM ALL?

by **Jason Arment**
Musalaheen

by **Tyler Atwood**
an electric sheep jumps to greener pasture

by **John W Barrios**
Here Comes the New Joy

by **Eirean Bradley**
the I in team
the little BIG book of go kill yourself

by **Suzanne Burns**
Boys

by **Calvero**
someday i'm going to marry Katy Perry
i want love so great it makes Nicholas Sparks cream in his
pants

by **Nikia Chaney**
us mouth

by **Leah Noble Davidson**
Poetic Scientifica
DOOR

by **Rory Douglas**
The Most Fun You'll Have at a Cage Fight

by **Brian S. Ellis**
American Dust Revisited
Often Go Awry

by **Greg Gerding**
The Burning Album of Lame
Venue Voyeurisms: Bars of San Diego
Loser Makes Good: Selected Poems 1994
Piss Artist: Selected Poems 1995-1999
The Idiot Parade: Selected Poems 2000-2005

by **Lauren Gilmore**
Outdancing the Universe

by **Rob Gray**
The Immaculate Collection / The Rhododendron and Camellia Year Book (1966)

by **Joseph Edwin Haeger**
Learn to Swim

by **Lindsey Kugler**
HERE.

by **Wryly T. McCutchen**
My Ugly & Other Love Snarls

by **Michael McLaughlin**
Countless Cinemas

by **Johnny No Bueno**
We Were Warriors
Concrete & Juniper

by **Isobel O'Hare**
all this can be yours (hardcover & paperback)

by **A.M. O'Malley**
Expecting Something Else

by **Stephen M. Park**
High & Dry
The Grass Is Greener

by **Christine Rice**
Swarm Theory

by **Thomas Lucky Richards**
Thirst for Beginners: Poems, Prose, and Quizzes

by **Liz Scott**
This Never Happened

by **Michael N. Thompson**
A Murder of Crows

by **Ellyn Touchette**
The Great Right-Here

by **Ran Walker**
Most of My Heroes Don't Appear on No Stamps

by **Sarah Xerta**
Nothing to Do with Me

edited by **Cam Awkward-Rich & Sam Sax**
The Dead Animal Handbook: An Anthology of Contemporary Poetry

edited by **Isobel O'Hare**
Erase the Patriarchy: An Anthology of Erasure Poetry

edited by **Greg Gerding**
2020* The Year of the Asterisk: An Anthology of American Essays

HELL PRESS
UNIVERSITY OF HELL PRESS